Landscape Architecture,
as Applied to the Wants of the West

ASLA CENTENNIAL REPRINT SERIES

*Country Life: A Handbook of Agriculture and Book of
Landscape Gardening* (1866)
Robert Morris Copeland

Landscape Architecture, as Applied to the Wants of the West (1873)
H. W. S. Cleveland

Charles Eliot, Landscape Architect (1902)
Charles W. Eliot

The Art of Landscape Architecture (1915)
Samuel Parsons Jr.

Prairie Spirit in Landscape Gardening (1915)
Wilhelm Miller

Landscape-Gardening (1920)
O. C. Simonds

The Spirit of the Garden (1923)
Martha Brookes Hutcheson

Book of Landscape Gardening (1926)
Frank Waugh

New Towns for Old (1927)
John Nolen

Landscape for Living (1950)
Garrett Eckbo

The series is underwritten by the Viburnum Foundation.

LANDSCAPE ARCHITECTURE,

AS APPLIED TO THE

WANTS OF THE WEST;

with an Essay on

Forest Planting on the Great Plains

H. W. S. CLEVELAND

Introduction by
Daniel J. Nadenicek
and
Lance M. Neckar

University of Massachusetts Press
Amherst and Boston

in association with

Library of American Landscape History
Amherst

Copyright © 2002 by University of Massachusetts Press
All rights reserved
Printed in the United States of America

LC 2002018018
ISBN 1-55849-330-1

Printed and bound by Thomson-Shore, Inc.

Library of Congress Cataloging-in-Publication Data

Cleveland, H. W. S. (Horace William Shaler), 1814–1900.
Landscape architecture, as applied to the wants of the West : with an
essay on forest planting on the Great Plains / H.W.S. Cleveland ;
introduction by Daniel J. Nadenicek and Lance M. Neckar.
— (American Society of Landscape Architects centennial reprint series)
Originally published: Chicago : Jansen, McClurg & Co., 1873.
Includes bibliographical references.
ISBN 1-55849-330-1 (cloth : alk. paper)
1. Landscape gardening—West (U.S.) 2. Landscape architecture—
West (U.S.) I. Library of American Landscape History. II. Centennial
reprint series.
SB472.32.U6 C64 2002
712'.0978—dc21

2002018018

British Library Cataloguing in Publication data are available.

PREFACE

The ASLA Centennial Reprint Series comprises a small library of influential historical books about American landscape architecture. The titles were selected by a committee of distinguished historians and practitioners who identified them as classics, important in shaping design, planting, planning, and stewardship practices in the field and still relevant today. Each is reprinted from the original edition and introduced by a new essay that provides historical and contemporary perspective. The project was undertaken by the Library of American Landscape History to commemorate the 1999 centennial of the American Society of Landscape Architects. The series is funded by the Viburnum Foundation, Rochester, New York.

Emblazoned across the cover of Horace William Shaler Cleveland's 1873 book, the words *Landscape Architecture* echoed the author's confidence in the profession to grapple with "issues of vital moment to the future of the country." Cleveland wrote his book to influence civic leaders and others who were laying out new American cities along the western rail expansion. Dismayed by the monotony and ugliness of these burgeoning towns, Cleveland proposed a more considered approach. In particular, he believed that parkways and park systems could provide green armatures for developing metropolises and that American civilization would flourish as a result. Many of these ideas proved influential and lasting.

Cleveland is one of the least understood of the giants of nineteenth-century American landscape design theory. His better-known colleagues, Andrew Jackson Downing, Charles Eliot, and Frederick Law Olmsted (for whom Cleveland briefly worked), have all been the subjects of in-depth biographies. By comparison, scholarship on Cleveland has been sparse, in large measure because he practiced in so many far-flung locales. The present essay by Daniel J. Nadenicek and Lance M. Neckar offers a particularly welcome rendering of Cleveland's life and career accomplishments. The authors provide new clarification of the impact and scope of his work—which included the design of cemeteries, residences, parks, suburbs, and entire cities—and the roots and expression of his distinctive "organic" approach to design. The brief text of Cleveland's book gains immeasurably from the background they furnish.

In the new introduction we read of Cleveland's Unitarian roots in Lancaster, Massachusetts, the family's brief residence in Cuba, and Cleveland's move back to New England, where he encountered novel ideas in a lively literary group that included Henry Wadsworth Longfellow. Cleveland then moved to New Jersey and became a scientific farmer (as Olmsted had), later returning to New England to found a landscape gardening partnership with Robert Morris Copeland. During these years he knew and was inspired by Ralph Waldo Emerson, who believed that landscape design should spring from the essential qualities and forms of nature. Nadenicek and Neckar amply document Emerson's influence on Cleveland's organic approach and discuss a prime example of it, Sleepy Hollow Cemetery in Concord, Massachusetts.

After the Civil War, Cleveland experimented with different careers and in 1869 moved to Chicago, likely as a consequence of railroad connections. There he set up a landscape architectural partnership with the civil engineer William Merchant Richardson French, brother of the famous sculptor. Cleveland began to lecture and write about the importance of thoughtful planning for the *Atlantic Monthly* and other publications. According to the authors, Cleveland believed that unchecked, rapid change throughout the American West would yield "a monotonous and characterless landscape that added nothing to the richness of life."

In the early 1870s, shortly before writing *Landscape Architecture, as Applied to the Wants of the West*, Cleveland began to travel to observe forestry experiments along the western rail lines and consider possible employment with one of the railroads. Nadenicek and Neckar hypothesize that "An Essay on Tree Planting on the Great Plains," which Cleveland appended to his book, may have been intended as an advertisement for his landscape architectural abilities.

Graceland Cemetery was among several projects Cleveland worked on in Chicago. He was followed there by another important practitioner, Ossian Cole Simonds, who was much influenced by Cleveland's nature-based approach to design. Through the example of the popular Chicago cemetery and the writings of Simonds and other prairie style practitioners, Cleveland's design ideas found gradual and widespread dissemination.

The final chapter of Cleveland's long career took place in Minneapolis, where he created the Minneapolis Parks, one of the most significant open-space systems in the United States. In its design Cleveland took full advantage of existing natural resources, including the system's signature landscape, Minnehaha Falls, which he protected from industrial development. Cleveland was thus among the first American landscape architects, in the words of the authors, to promote "a conservation ethic as an appropriate companion to landscape intervention."

Cleveland's impact on his profession extended well beyond the example of his built works. The progressive attitudes he espoused, primarily in *Landscape Architecture, as Applied to the Wants of the West*, helped lay the foundation for modern city planning as developed by Frederick Law Olmsted Jr., John Nolen, and other early twentieth-century practitioners. Cleveland thereby played a significant role in redefining the scope of landscape architecture's focus—from agriculture, horticulture, and pleasure grounds to conservation and the design of park systems and entire cities. *Landscape Architecture* bears witness to the strength and creativity of his vision.

To vitalize the connection between H. W. S. Cleveland's ideas and contemporary issues of design, land use, and stewardship, the Library of American Landscape History has invited the Center for Landscape Studies in Landscape History of the Pennsylvania State University and the University of Minnesota College of Architecture and Landscape Architecture to collaborate with LALH on educational programming. We hope

that this collaboration results in Cleveland's insights' reaching
wide audiences and assisting practitioners in facing new design and planning challenges.

> Robin Karson, Executive Director
> Library of American Landscape History
> Amherst, Massachusetts

The Library of American Landscape History, Inc., a nonprofit
corporation, produces books and exhibitions about American
landscape history. Its mission is to educate and thereby promote
thoughtful stewardship of the land.

LIBRARY of

AMERICAN
LANDSCAPE
HISTORY

FIGURE 1. Horace William Shaler Cleveland, 1882.
William H. Tishler Collection.

INTRODUCTION
TO THE
REPRINT EDITION

Daniel J. Nadenicek
and
Lance M. Neckar

"I am not aware that any writer has ever attempted to apply the principles of the art [of landscape architecture], on the scale . . . required to meet the demands which devolve upon us, yet I am confident that no one will deny that it involves issues of vital moment to the future of the country."[1] Thus, Horace William Shaler Cleveland (1814–1900) (fig. 1) concluded his introductory chapter of *Landscape Architecture, as Applied to the Wants of the West; with an Essay on Forest Planting on the Great Plains* (1873). He had recently moved to Chicago where he hoped to make a significant difference in shaping much of the western half of the nation undergoing rapid settlement along the developing rail network. He was convinced that the new profession of landscape architecture needed to expand the scope as well as the scale of its practice, if it were successfully to engage the needs of post–Civil War America.

Landscape Architecture, as Applied to the Wants of the West was written at a watershed moment in the nation's history and in Cleveland's career. By the 1870s pressure for change, long held in check by the political realities of antebellum America (uncertainty about slavery and an incomplete rail network, for example), burst forth with great force. During that period, politicos, railroad entrepreneurs, land speculators, and other missionaries of change worked at a feverish pace to transform the western half of the nation. While many subscribed to the "manifest destiny" spirit of the age, few could envision the future form and appearance of the landscape under construction. By 1873 Cleveland held a clear sense of the profession's potential to plan and design for the future wants of civilization. In writing his book, he created a typology of actions across scales to create a continuous framework, or armature, for future growth. From that point of view, the book is a mission statement with a detailed design agenda for what might be accomplished in various kinds of projects from suburbs to park systems on the rapidly developing lands in the nation's vast interior.

At the same time that Cleveland presented this plan for the hinterland, he was dubious about his own future. Landscape architecture was so new in the early 1870s that despite his growing practice it was difficult for him to act with surety about the economic potential of the new profession.[2] It was also a period of intense land speculation related to railroad development. Thus, Cleveland's book should also be viewed as a promotional document—a search for work along multiple paths. Cleveland reasoned that he might be successful in developing his career as a landscape designer in the new region, but he might also work in the employ of a railroad, managing tree-planting efforts on the Great Plains. The "Essay on Forest Planting on the Great Plains," then, while thematically linked to Cleveland's desire to shape cities and towns, can also be read as a separate essay and an indication that he was hedging his bets, in an uncertain land economy, about his future course.[3] In any case, Cleveland did not separate forestry from the comprehensive agenda of landscape architecture; forestry as a specialization would not emerge until a later period of professionalization.

Horace Cleveland was Andrew Jackson Downing's contemporary and, after Downing's untimely death in 1852, joined other pioneer landscape designers—Frederick Law Olmsted, Calvert Vaux, and Robert Morris Copeland—in establishing the mission and agenda of the new profession. Cleveland has often been portrayed merely as Olmsted's protégé.[4] Cleveland's practice in landscape design, however, which began in 1854 in partnership with Copeland, predates Olmsted's Greensward plan for New York's Central Park by three years. In the realm of landscape aesthetics, both Cleveland and Olmsted should be credited with creative innovations that shaped the urbanization of the United States in the last half of the nineteenth century. Cleveland did not travel as widely as Olmsted, and he was greatly influenced by American literary explorations of landscape. Though both men looked to Ralph Waldo Emerson, Cleveland translated the transcendentalist's aesthetic musings into an organic approach that differed from Olmsted's naturalistic style, which also incorporated principles of composition derived from the English aesthetic theorist John Ruskin.[5]

This introduction places *Landscape Architecture, as Applied to the Wants of the West* within the context of Cleveland's evolving career, as an important manifesto on the role of landscape architecture in a changing nation. Olmsted had not been able to write a book about his approach to the new profession—rather his much-imitated design work, more than his eloquently argued written apologies, became the text of his ideas. Cleveland's book is the one publication from the period offering a clear vantage on the role of the new profession in "arranging land [for] . . . the varied wants of civilization."[6]

Horace Cleveland was born in Lancaster, Massachusetts, in 1814, the third son of Richard Jeffry and Dorcas Hiller Cleveland. His father's seafaring fortune provided the means for the family to purchase a rural estate in Lancaster,[7] and thus the elder Cleveland emulated other entrepreneurs who derived wealth from the sea while seeking solace and moral solidity through an engagement with the land.[8]

Lancaster as a specific location for rural life was of interest to the Clevelands because of its growing Unitarian population. Unitarianism during this period injected the older puritan morality and hierarchy with a new optimistic spirit based on the belief that human advance through individual effort should be the goal of society. This individual moral advance, known as "character development," was to be managed by a group of societal superintendents—those with money, intellect, or artistic prowess, for example—who believed it their mission to improve the human condition. The focus of those benevolent efforts in society ranged from religious writing to agricultural study and educational experiment.[9] Unitarian philosophy had direct physical results in the construction of schools, museums, libraries, orphanages, and eventually public parks.

The Cleveland family was at the leading edge of the new religion. Dorcas Cleveland later authored a number of Unitarian pamphlets, and after the move to Lancaster, Richard Cleveland assisted in the construction of a new Unitarian house of worship, a church designed by the renowned architect of the Massachusetts State House, Charles Bulfinch. The Cleveland family also chartered a school to prepare young boys to attend Harvard. Dorcas Cleveland organized and managed the Lancaster Academy, as it was called, based upon the principles of Johann Heinrich Pestalozzi, a Swiss education theorist. Along with the classics, the school's innovative curriculum emphasized landscape study and observation. Two early teachers at the school, Jared Sparks, a historian, Unitarian leader, and later Harvard president, and George Barrell Emerson, an educator, naturalist, and cousin of Ralph Waldo Emerson, would influence Horace's developing worldview and, especially in the case of George Emerson, his practical approach to landscape intervention.[10] A number of students who graduated from the Lancaster Academy later made significant contributions to society. Horatio Greenough, the sculptor and art theorist, for example, conceived organic aesthetic theories in concert with Ralph Waldo Emerson. As we shall see, those theories had a direct influence on Cleveland's practice of landscape architecture.

In the late 1820s, Richard Cleveland accepted a diplomatic position and the family moved to Havana, Cuba. There, Horace developed a deeper understanding of the landscape. He was particularly intrigued by Cuban horticultural practices such as mulching techniques used on coffee plantations, and he no doubt became aware of theories about the healthful effects of tropical landscapes.[11] He later applied those practical and theoretical views of landscape first as a scientific farmer and then as a landscape designer.

In the 1830s, Cleveland went west, perhaps to survey undeveloped lands in Illinois for eastern commercial interests and land speculators.[12] He also taught school there, and "board[ed] round with pupils" and had shooting matches with the "big boys" at noon.[13] Years later Cleveland recalled the wild region as a "dream-land," suggesting the long-lasting inspiration of the experience. After returning to Massachusetts in the late 1830s, Cleveland stayed with brother Henry and his wife Sarah Perkins Cleveland at their Jamaica Plain home. Henry was a well-known scholar and teacher and met regularly with a literary group known as the Five of Clubs, which included George Hillard, later a well-known parks advocate, orator, and jurist; Cornelius Felton, a classical scholar and future president of Harvard; Charles Sumner, destined to become the fiery antislavery senator from Massachusetts; and Henry Wadsworth Longfellow.[14] Through his brother Horace was accepted into this elite literary circle, and he was particularly influenced by Longfellow.[15] During the years that Cleveland met with the Five of Clubs, Longfellow was completing his novel *Hyperion*, a central theme of which was human improvement through character development. Cleveland followed Longfellow's career until the poet's death in 1882. (He wrote to Longfellow in 1881 quoting words from *Hyperion* as essential to his own life philosophy.)[16] In the 1850s, Longfellow more fully developed the theme of human improvement in an

American context of manifest destiny in his classic, *The Song of Hiawatha,* which inspired Cleveland's later design of Minnehaha Park in Minneapolis, the major pilgrimage site related to the epic poem.

In the years that followed those early literary encounters, Cleveland set out to fulfill his civic responsibility in the field of scientific agriculture. In the early 1840s he married Maryann Dwinel of Maine and established Oatlands, a scientific farm in Burlington, New Jersey, where his agricultural experiments afforded him the opportunity to communicate the power of landscape improvement to enrich the lives of rural Americans and fellow market gardeners. He and other scientific farmers wrote about the care and maintenance of the landscape in journals such as Downing's *Horticulturist* and Simon Brown's *New England Farmer.* Cleveland's writings were often practical: he became a well-known authority on the uses of mulch to preserve moisture in planted areas, he studied hydrology and drainage, and during the 1840s, he became an expert in pomology and experimented with woodlot management. Those varied experiences were useful to him when he began his landscape design practice.

Cleveland's scientific farming experiments and writing in the 1840s and 1850s were also intended for social purposes. America was still largely a rural nation, but the state of agriculture was poor, especially compared with that of England and other European nations. For economic reasons, many New England farmers left their farms to work in developing industrial centers or for the promise of richer lands to the west.[17] Cleveland's task and that of other scientific farmers, country gentlemen, and country-life writers was to help provide the means and the motivation for New England farmers to stay on their farms, for it was believed that rural life with its close association to the reflective and restorative capacities of the land was a morally superior life.[18]

In 1854, however, Cleveland's search for a benevolent calling took another turn when he formed a landscape design partnership in Massachusetts with Robert Morris Copeland. The transition from scientific agriculture was gradual; in the first years of their partnership they offered both design services and agricultural advice.[19] Early commissions with a scientific farming emphasis include the design for the grounds of the state farm at Westborough, Massachusetts, and tree-planting experiments with the naturalist George Barrell Emerson for his home near Boston Harbor.[20]

In the early years of their evolving practice, Cleveland and Copeland also designed private estates (including the Samuel Colt estate in Hartford, Connecticut), cemeteries (Oak Grove Cemetery in Gloucester, Massachusetts, for example), and small parks with an eye toward physical and conceptual linkages and assurance of the usefulness of such work to society at large. During this period, Cleveland developed a strong aesthetic and philosophical base for his work. Through George Emerson, he was personally acquainted with Ralph Waldo Emerson, the preeminent transcendentalist poet/philosopher, and held his writing in high regard.[21] Emerson occasionally traveled in the same horticultural and scientific farming circles as Cleveland, and served on various local committees, including the Concord Cemetery board that hired Cleveland and Copeland to design

FIGURE 2. Sleepy Hollow Cemetery gate, no longer extant. *Concord, Massachusetts, Free Public Library.*

Sleepy Hollow Cemetery (fig. 2). Emerson frequently sought ways of grounding his philosophical musings in action; his theoretical explorations of aesthetics were motivated by a practical concern for finding a source of artistic creation befitting the American spirit and landscape.

Cleveland's knowledge of Emerson's aesthetic theories was particularly important to his understanding of the role of nature in design. Emerson's organic principle maintained that design should spring from the essential qualities and forms of nature. During the 1830s and 1840s, Emerson and the sculptor Horatio Greenough wrote of the need for an American aesthetic untainted by the decadent and opulent forms of the European-influenced Renaissance and baroque styles that were popular sources for revivalists in all of the fine and useful arts.[22] In suggesting that artistic forms should be derived directly from the American scene, Emerson equated beauty with truth and showed contempt for borrowed European form and all unnecessary artificial embellishment.[23]

There is considerable evidence of Cleveland's attachment to Emerson's organic aesthetic. He used language similar to Emerson's in describing his aesthetic charge when he published "Landscape Gardening" for the *Christian Examiner* in 1855.[24] In *A Few Words on the Central Park* (1856) he and Copeland suggested in Emersonian fashion that the artist in the landscape should forgo the use of "artificial embellishment," while looking directly to the landscape to "render to the popular mind . . . [the lessons found in the] rude cliffs and . . . moss covered rocks, and the beauty of the graceful forms in which the hills and fields were moulded by the hand of God."[25] The landscape architect's role was to comprehend the essence of those natural elements engaging them with a light hand out of respect for the creator (or "oversoul," to use Emerson's word). In this setting superfluous ornament was deemed inappropriate to the task of landscape architecture.

The best evidence of Cleveland's affinity for Emerson's aesthetic concepts is Sleepy Hollow Cemetery in Concord, Massachusetts, designed by Cleveland and Copeland in 1855 (fig. 3). The cemetery was carefully fitted to a natural amphitheater where common and native plants were planted and maintained, providing a "picturesque effect of familiar shrubs . . . [and] thorns."[26] Cleveland and Copeland's design of this cemetery, the final resting place of Emerson, Nathaniel Hawthorne, Henry David Thoreau, A. Bronson Alcott, Louisa May Alcott, and Elizabeth Palmer Peabody, clearly reflects transcendentalist thinking and an Emersonian worldview. Most revealing of all of

FIGURE 3. Natural amphitheater at Sleepy Hollow Cemetery, ca.
1870. *Concord, Massachusetts, Free Public Library*.

Emerson's musings on the art of landscape design is his "Address to the Inhabitants of Concord at the Consecration of Sleepy Hollow" delivered on September 29, 1855 (fig. 4). It is likely that Cleveland and Copeland were present as Emerson articulated the artistic vision and design intent for the cemetery. Emerson told the audience that the "lay and the look of the land" suggested the design and that art was employed only to bring out the site's "natural advantages."(fig. 5)[27]

Cleveland's organic aesthetic differed from Olmsted's, whose landscape experiments, inspired by Ruskin, were somewhat removed from the existing natural settings of his designs.[28] Cleveland's search for an organic approach mapped the largely uncharted territory of American picturesque landscape design.[29] From that perspective, Cleveland was a pioneer and an inventor in his efforts to test the boundaries of an organic approach in American landscape architecture.

In his consecration address, Emerson pointed out that

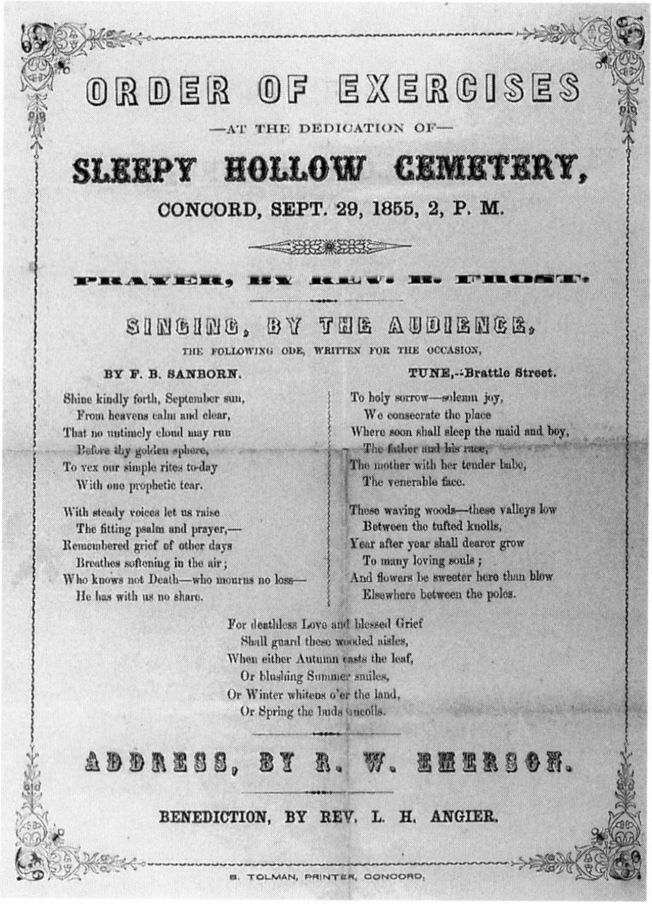

ORDER OF EXERCISES

—AT THE DEDICATION OF—

SLEEPY HOLLOW CEMETERY,

CONCORD, SEPT. 29, 1855, 2, P. M.

PRAYER, BY REV. B. FROST.

SINGING, BY THE AUDIENCE,

THE FOLLOWING ODE, WRITTEN FOR THE OCCASION,

BY F. B. SANBORN. TUNE,—Brattle Street.

Shine kindly forth, September sun,
From heavens calm and clear,
That no untimely cloud may run
Before thy golden sphere,
To vex our simple rites to-day
With one prophetic tear.

With steady voices let us raise
The fitting psalm and prayer,—
Remembered grief of other days
Breathes softening in the air;
Who knows not Death—who mourns no loss—
He has with us no share.

To holy sorrow—solemn joy,
We consecrate the place
Where soon shall sleep the maid and boy,
The father and his race,
The mother with her tender babe,
The venerable face.

These waving woods—these valleys low
Between the tufted knolls,
Year after year shall dearer grow
To many loving souls;
And flowers be sweeter here than blow
Elsewhere between the poles.

For deathless Love and blessed Grief
Shall guard these wooded aisles,
When either Autumn casts the leaf,
Or blushing Summer smiles,
Or Winter whitens o'er the land,
Or Spring the buds uncoils.

ADDRESS, BY R. W. EMERSON.

BENEDICTION, BY REV. L. H. ANGIER.

B. TOLMAN, PRINTER, CONCORD.

FIGURE 4. Order of Exercises for the dedication of Sleepy Hollow Cemetery with Emerson's address highlighted. *Concord, Massachusetts, Free Public Library*.

FIGURE 5. Ridge walk at Sleepy Hollow Cemetery. *Photograph by Lance M. Neckar.*

Sleepy Hollow was a community park, a place of recreation for the Concord community—for gatherings, "games for the school children and for education."[30] The construction of this picturesque public park a few years before Central Park represents perceptive thinking on the part of Concord officials, but even more visionary was that Sleepy Hollow was intended as part of a public open-space system. In his consecration address, Emerson indicated that the cemetery was but one part in a larger system of public spaces composing a town-country continuum (fig. 6).[31] A number of factors likely contributed to open-space linkages in Concord, but much credit belongs to Sleepy Hollow's designers, who, one year later, were making similar suggestions for such linkages on Commonwealth Avenue in Boston's Back Bay.[32] Cleveland and Copeland conceived Commonwealth Avenue for the recreational use of adjoining neighborhoods, but also as a means of connecting the Boston

FIGURE 6. Pine-bordered path at the edge of Sleepy Hollow Cemetery. *Concord, Massachusetts, Free Public Library.*

Common and Public Garden to recreational spaces on the city's periphery.[33]

Both Cleveland and Copeland continued to explore the power and potential of linking public landscapes, but even before the Civil War intervened, they amicably separated. During the war, Copeland served as a major in the Union army and Cleveland "took an active part in organizing and instructing rifle clubs," and possibly training Union sharpshooters.[34] For Cleveland the formative years were of vital importance in preparing him to take on grander challenges after the Civil War. As he moved forward with his life and career he remained the stalwart New Englander committed to guide the movement of American civilization with missionary zeal. After his move west his nebulous philosophy coalesced as the organic approach, once applied, became directly effectual in projects that shaped the new land.

After the Civil War, Cleveland followed a circuitous path to the major move of his life—his relocation to Chicago in 1869. In the late 1860s he tested a number of career opportunities. He continued pursuing an interest in firearms, considered starting a design practice in the nation's capital, perhaps designed a community near Tarrytown, New York, and assisted Olmsted and Vaux during the construction of Prospect Park in Brooklyn, New York.[35] Cleveland's close association with Olmsted during this period may have influenced his move west. Certainly both men were aware of the opportunities and challenges of planning for settlement in the nation's interior. Olmsted, of course, also worked in the Midwest—he and

Vaux were hired to design Riverside, Illinois, a new suburban community near Chicago, in 1869, and to prepare the plan for the South Parks in the city in 1870–71—and may have suggested to Cleveland that there was great potential for a landscape design practice in the region.[36]

It is probable, however, that the impetus for the move was an opportunity that surfaced as a consequence of railroad connections. Through his brother Henry's marriage into the James Perkins family, Horace became acquainted with John Murray Forbes, the president of the Chicago, Burlington and Quincy Railroad (CB&Q). Forbes, who was James Perkins's nephew and Emerson's brother-in-law and a noted Unitarian, had learned Yankee business practices in his uncle's China trade counting house. Cleveland's relationship with railroad leaders, including Charles Perkins, a nephew of Forbes and later president of the CB&Q, for example, provided him a clear vantage on the great design potential created by opening the West to commerce and settlement.[37] Some of Cleveland's most notable commissions, such as Robbins Addition (1870) in Hinsdale, Illinois, illustrated in Cleveland's pamphlet *A Few Hints on Landscape Gardening in the West* (1871), and the Highland Cemetery in Junction City, Kansas (ca. 1871), stem from connections to the CB&Q and its western extensions (fig. 7).[38]

Although the development of the continental railroad network offered significant opportunities to superintend the shaping of western communities, the haste of railroad construction caused numerous problems. For example, building, operating, and maintaining the railroads and the settlements along them led to significant deforestation.[39] Cleveland espe-

SUBURBS

OF CHICAGO,

ON THE CHICAGO, BURLINGTON & QUINCY R. R.

ILLUSTRATED.

O, when I am safe in my silvan home,
I mock at the pride of Greece and Rome. — *Emerson.*

FIGURE 7. *Suburbs of Chicago on the Chicago, Burlington & Quincy R. R.*, ca. 1875, which includes Cleveland's Hinsdale project. *Chicago Historical Society.*

cially detested the railroad practice of laying out gridded communities without regard for the existing topographical features.[40] He believed that such practices, driven by speed and efficiency rather than thoughtful planning, were bound to create a less than civil civilization. To Cleveland those railroad practices were only a symptom of a larger problem. Future difficulties as well as great potential were linked to the unprecedented celerity of change induced by the formation and investment of capital.

In 1870, a year after his move to Chicago, Cleveland wrote in an article for the *Atlantic Monthly*, "The peopling of a great extent of wild country by immigration from over-crowded nations is like the flood of waters from pent-up reservoirs into a vast interior basin."[41] Chicago was emerging as the linchpin of the nation, effectively linking the East to the prairie hinterland, and the alluring potential of that western "dream-land" with an apparently endless supply of fertile soil and boundless resources attracted zealots of change by the trainload. Cleveland believed that swift change based only on expediency and market forces would yield a monotonous and characterless landscape; he was interested in bringing thoughtful design and planning to a haphazard pattern of settlement.

In Chicago, Cleveland formed a loose partnership with William Merchant Richardson French, brother of the sculptor Daniel Chester French and later director of the Chicago Art Institute.[42] He and French designed the community of Highland Park, Illinois (1869–74). Cleveland's office was rapidly becoming a regional entity. Cleveland made an addition to Graceland Cemetery (fig. 8) in Chicago in 1870, probably

FIGURE 8. Madlener plot, Graceland Cemetery, ca. 1880. E. D. Carr album, *Chicago Historical Society*.

with Samuel Greeley as his surveyor. In 1871 he had published "A Few Hints" as a companion piece to French's "The Relation of Engineering to Landscape Gardening."[43] In this period he designed the Brookside Addition (ca. 1870–72), a subdivision in Indianapolis, Indiana, for the Fletcher family, who are often mentioned in his letters to French as well as cited as endorsers of his work in "Hints." Similar endorsements came from clients in Cedar Rapids and Des Moines, Iowa. These commissioned works and those tracts set the stage for the publication of *Landscape Architecture, as Applied to the Wants of the West; with an Essay on Forest Planting on the Great Plains.* In the year of the book, 1873, Cleveland designed

Drexel Boulevard and reconceived the scheme for the South (Washington) Park, both for the Chicago South Parks Commission (fig. 9). Using native and common plants on a minimally graded site, consistent with the organic aesthetic, which matched the practical wishes of the clients and his experiences on other projects in New England and the West, Cleveland transformed the design and reduced the budget impact of the Olmsted and Vaux scheme for a *plaisance* with subtropical effects.

Concurrent with writing his book, Cleveland and his partner French laid out the streets and lots of Highland Park—later advertised as "a vast natural park"—on a landscape of deep ravines opening to Lake Michigan (fig. 10).[44] This design and others we know that French drew and executed in the field from surveys of spot elevations on fifty-foot grids were masterpieces of designed topography. The survey allowed the designers to fit the mixed curvilinear and gridiron plan of streets and lots to the rough landforms and the railroad. The design preserved the ravines in a wild, though largely accessible state, and the suburban community thus perches on bluffs cut through by ephemeral stream courses to the beaches. Cleveland and French's design preserved the ravines by two devices: some were held as public parks, while the majority were shared by neighbors whose house lots were defined by buildable bluff-top sites and rear boundaries that run along the centerlines of the ravines.[45] In effect Cleveland and French conceived the ravines as naturalized commons and intended that individual home grounds would, therefore, borrow from the shared values of a connective public realm. Cleveland's ideas were influenced by French's sophisticated understand-

FIGURE 9. Washington Park, Chicago South Parks, ca. 1873–75, view opposite Unity and New England Churches showing large, transplanted trees and crew with lawn mower. *Chicago Historical Society*.

ing of natural topography, his own organic aesthetic, and an overall commitment to community built on a civic framework (much more than a mere collection of individual estates).[46]

It was in his conceptual work on urban centers that Cleveland most fully developed the idea of a system of public

HIGHLAND PARK!

This beautiful Suburban Village is located on the Lake Shore, seventeen miles North of Chicago, on the Chicago & Milwaukee R. R., over which *Trains pass every hour in the day.* The Land for miles in every direction from Highland Park Station, is very high, being seventy-five feet above Lake Michigan at the Lake Shore; and is, in fact, as its name indicates, one vast

NATURAL PARK,

covered with a magnificent growth of trees of every size and variety. The Village now contains *One Thousand People,* all *first-class families.* The houses, so far built, are beautiful in architecture as well as substantial in construction, and imparts to the view an air of comfort seldom met with.

BOILVIN'S ADDITION

lies four blocks West of the Depot, is beautifully layed out with spacious Avenues and Streets, and so scientifically Subdivided by circles and curves that all the Avenues centre at *RIDGELAND PARK,* which gives a frontage of **4,500** feet, or **150** lots, overlooking the *PARK.* Each lot is covered with natural forest trees, from two to eight inches in diameter. There is, in fact, no Suburban Town within reach of Chicago that presents so many attractions and advantages for residence property, at present, as

HIGHLAND PARK!

Lots are offered at the low price of **two hundred and fifty dollars,** on easy terms.

20848 Apply to

C. W. DEAN,

Room 14, NO. 100 Washington Street.

NOTE.—The Town is entirely free from those business Houses, called Saloons.

FIGURE 10. Highland Park advertisement for building lots, featuring the words "natural park." *Chicago Historical Society.*

parks as a civic framework. As we have seen, Copeland and
Cleveland had experimented with the idea of designing linked
public open spaces as early as 1855. After the Civil War they
wrote about the idea of a connected system for Boston in published tracts and editorials.[47] Cleveland advocated such linkages in *The Public Grounds of Chicago: How to Give Them
Character and Expression* (1869), a piece written as much about
Boston as Chicago.[48] And in 1872 Copeland further developed
his thinking in *The Most Beautiful City in America: Essay and
Plan for the Improvement of the City of Boston*, which Cleveland
positively commented on in his own book.[49] Cleveland understood that twenty years of urbanization in America following
his work on Sleepy Hollow and Commonwealth Avenue had
verified his hypotheses about the value of tree-lined, parklike
linear connective spaces in cities.

Among other factors in Cleveland's thinking was the model
of the second imperial incarnation of Paris, as he understood it
from reading William Robinson's *Parks and Gardens and Promenades of Paris* (1868). In this book, the Irish-born garden author
reported on the delights of the new bourgeois public landscapes
of the city. Engineer Georges Haussmann had remade the
street fabric of Paris based on the imperial model of Rome
under Sixtus V. To this new set of multi-modal streets, J. C. A.
Alphand had added a park system of multiple types and scales.
By the early 1870s, Cleveland was promoting Robinson's book
to his prairie clients in Chicago, St. Paul, and Minneapolis; and
he mentioned it in the book as a source of his ideas for a civic
armature of larger and smaller parks connected by boulevards.[50]
Cleveland's initial work on Drexel Boulevard and the South

Parks in 1873 gave him important technical experience and a prophetic window onto the value of linked systems in the fast-growing cities of the Midwest. It also clarified for him the importance of developing a like-minded group of civic supporters for such broad action.

Cleveland was well aware that such developing cities as Chicago were inextricably embedded in a large regional landscape in need of thoughtful planning.[51] While several commissions resulted from his railroad connections, Cleveland also considered the possibility of direct employment with two of those railroads. He was offered the job of managing tree-planting efforts for the western extension of the Chicago, Burlington and Quincy—an offer he ultimately rejected—and he actively pursued a similar position with the Northern Pacific Railroad but without success.[52] During the early 1870s, Cleveland traveled west along the rails to observe forestry efforts, studied the tree-planting experiments of the Kansas Pacific Railroad, read George Perkins Marsh's *Man and Nature* (1864), and followed congressional action on the subject. The potential importance of trees to the largely treeless Great Plains was part of a national debate during the early 1870s. Arbor Day was first observed in Nebraska in 1870, and a vote on the first Timber Culture Act was pending in Congress when Cleveland's book was in press.[53] Furthermore, every railroad operation with which Cleveland was familiar understood that the massive planting of trees was of vital importance to future profits.

All of those early western commissions and experiences allowed Cleveland to test and develop concepts before writing *Landscape Architecture, as Applied to the Wants of the West*.

With the publication of the book in 1873 his major precepts were developed and clarified.⁵⁴ The words *Landscape Architecture* were prominently displayed in gilded type on the cover of the book. While the cover design may have been out of Cleveland's control, it does speak to his perspective on the emerging profession. In his preface Cleveland stated that the term was "only figuratively expressive of the art it is used to designate."⁵⁵ He also suggested that it was the best name available to reflect immense charge of the new profession—the scale and scope of its interventions extending well beyond traditional landscape gardening. The book was both a manifesto for the future and a practical handbook on its making. At times it is clearly promotional, as if Cleveland were trying to convince developers, politicians, and railroad entrepreneurs to consider his services. At other times the writing, like a good sermon, resonates with a holy intonation of service and civic responsibility for the benefit of civilization.

The book called for quick action in response to the impending crisis caused by the rapid deployment of population across the continent.⁵⁶ Massive unplanned change was sure to destroy natural and scenic wonders, creating a sterile, mundane world—a "workshop" as he called it in another context.⁵⁷ Fortunately, landscape architecture was a profession equipped to offer solutions; he defined it as *"the art of arranging land so as to adapt it most conveniently, economically and gracefully to any of the varied wants of civilization."*⁵⁸ To realize that charge, Cleveland articulated physical design strategies related to various landscape types—including the suburban domestic grounds, the suburban addition, the town plan, the park, the parkway, and the boulevard—advocating the organic aesthetic that new places must be carefully built on existing conditions. Emulating Emerson, he reminded the reader that artificial embellishment could only detract from those natural features "conferring an air of ostentatious display."[59]

The book's organization is loosely based on scale, moving from residential design early in the book to the making of the city and its many component parts, and ultimately arriving at his proposal for the Great Plains. While understanding the interconnectedness of those landscape types, Cleveland offered specific advice for what might be accomplished for each type. For the city, he was concerned with the park, the park system, and the suburban addition. For the greater landscape lying in between and beyond the principal cities, Cleveland suggested a more enlightened way to plan towns and emphasized the importance of planting forests. It is easy to understand why he offered a forestry essay at the conclusion of his book given the national debate on the importance of tree planting and Cleveland's developing expertise on the subject.

At the heart of Cleveland's book is his plan for a public open-space system for urban centers to support the making of American civilization in the West.[60] The city was intended to grow on an armature of linked parks and boulevards. Such a system allowed for pleasant and efficient movement through the city and provided park amenities for neighborhood communities.[61] At the outer reaches of the city, Cleveland envisioned parklike suburbs organically designed to fit the land. In discussing this plan he again expressed great urgency, using Chicago as an example where many opportunities for sound planning had been lost.[62]

Horace Cleveland, the proper New Englander, still won-

dered about the exact shape of his career. He walked the bus-
tling streets of Chicago—a city alive with movement, a gath-
ering place of old-world peoples and the nexus of a new world
under construction. While his unwavering belief in the need
for social guidance, derived from his nurture in the ideals of
New England, remained solid, his personal role in the process
was yet to be determined. He was making money as a landscape architect but was still uncertain that the practice as he
had defined it in most of his projects would make a career.
Major events beyond his control exacerbated the uncertainty.
In 1871 much of Chicago burned to the ground including
Cleveland's office and most of its contents.[63] Then in 1873 the
nation slipped into a severe financial panic in large measure
due to overzealous railroad and real-estate speculation. Amid
that uncertainty and tumult he continued to explore the important ideas that would form the central themes of his book.
After the Panic and the publication of the book, Cleveland
executed important commissions and made significant contacts. He and French designed Oakland Cemetery (1873–74)
(fig. 11) in St. Paul, Minnesota, and the Evergreen Cemetery
(1874), in Menomonie, Wisconsin. In 1874 Cleveland also designed the community of St. Anthony Park between St. Paul
and Minneapolis, and Eastwood Cemetery in his hometown
of Lancaster, Massachusetts.

   Cleveland's nurture in New England and his early experiments in landscape intervention provided a solid conceptual
and practical base for engaging that expansive landscape, but
there was no way for him to know in 1873 the precise nature
of his own involvement in implementing this paper plan. Of
all the partially tested concepts contained in his book, the idea

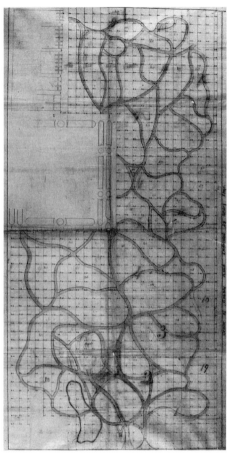

FIGURE 11. Topographical survey and roadway design, Oakland Cemetery, St. Paul, Minnesota, designed by Cleveland and French, 1873. *Oakland Cemetery Archives*.

of connecting public spaces was the most innovative and successfully implemented in the years that followed. With other societal superintendents influenced by the ideals of New England, Cleveland was later able to design and implement his crowning achievement, the Minneapolis Park System.

In the years following the publication of the book, Cleveland's gaze (both into his personal future and the future of the emerging profession) came into clear focus. The panic of 1873 halted the construction of the railroads as well as any related forestry efforts.[64] And the field of forestry itself matured. John Wesley Powell's 1874 report to Congress suggested that interventions in the arid regions of the nation should take on a very different character from those in the eastern states. Ubiquitous tree planting everywhere in the drier regions was considered neither practical nor desirable. By the 1880s, the idea that massive tree plantings could substantially alter the climate was generally criticized as unscientific. Furthermore, during the same years, the railroads were increasingly depicted as forest destroyers.[65]

Cleveland distanced himself from a direct professional interest in forestry, and his opportunities in landscape architecture increased in number, geographic scope, and complexity. He worked on several projects during the late 1870s and 1880s—Roger Williams Park, Providence, Rhode Island (1878), Natural Bridge, Virginia (1885), the Jekyll Island Club, Brunswick, Georgia (1886), Washburn Park subdivision, Minneapolis, Minnesota (1886), the Minnesota Soldiers Home, Minneapolis (ca. 1887), Como Park and Summit Avenue, St. Paul, Minnesota (1889), and the Omaha Park System (beginning in 1889),

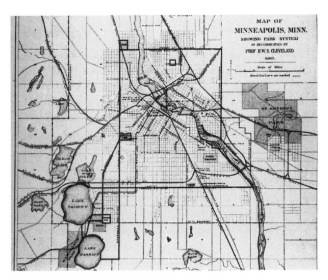

FIGURE 12. Cleveland's plan for the Minneapolis park system in *Suggestions for a System of Parks and Parkways for the City of Minneapolis* (1883).

to name a few—but it was in Minneapolis that he most successfully and thoroughly converted his written plan to physical reality.

Cleveland made his initial contacts in St. Paul and Minneapolis in 1872. He resided in Chicago when the Minneapolis work began in 1883 but moved to the Twin Cities during the early years of construction. He provided a schematic diagram (fig. 12) and discussed the plan in *Suggestions for a System of Parks and Parkways for the City of Minneapolis* (1883), and he also offered watercolor plans (themselves schematic) of most of the parks proposed for the system.[66] The construction superintendent William Morse Berry, who had worked with him in Chicago, served as Cleveland's lieutenant and helped him make detailed decisions in the field.

Cleveland was successful in Minneapolis in great measure because he operated with kindred spirits. He was introduced to the city by the founding president of the University of Minnesota, William Watts Folwell, later a leader of the Parks Commission.[67] He worked with other New Englanders—including Berry, from Maine—who shared his social perspective. Charles M. Loring, another Maine native and president of the local civic improvement association, was made chairman of the new park commission in the same year that Cleveland was retained to design the park and parkway system for the city.[68] The system combined elements of built and natural form, draped over the city's hills and around its lakes and along the Mississippi River. Cleveland successfully linked boulevards, small neighborhood parks of Parisian derivation, prairie ponds with wild islands, and lake-edge parkways (fig. 13). The core of this system stretched from a small Central Park (today named Loring Park) along the edges of bluffs and lakes to the south of the downtown. The early work on the parks proceeded so rapidly that some important design decisions were actually made on-site. While excavating a small lake in Central Park, Loring stopped the work when he saw that an island that had been left might be an attractive addition to the park. Cleveland agreed, and the wild island was planted with native shrubs; the effort was noted in a brief article in the magazine *Garden and Forest*.[69]

Work on the Minneapolis park system continued through the 1880s. If that system was Cleveland's greatest accomplish-

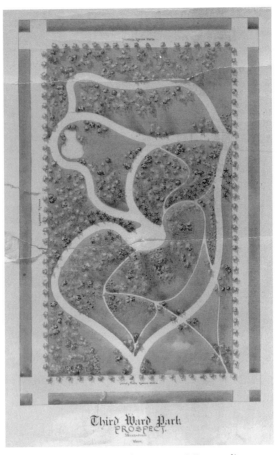

Third Ward Park
PROSPECT.
Minneapolis.
Minn.

FIGURE 13. Third Ward Park, Prospect, Minneapolis, Minnesota, 1883–86, a neighborhood park recalling Parc des Buttes Chaumont, Paris. *Hennepin County Historical Society.*

FALLS OF MINNEHAHA.

FIGURE 14. Engraving of Minnehaha Falls from *Picturesque America, or the Land We Live In* (1874).

ment, Minnehaha Park stands as its signature landscape (fig. 14). Cleveland and Henry Wadsworth Longfellow, as we have seen, held a shared philosophy about improvement for society. In *The Song of Hiawatha* (1855) Longfellow suggested the potency of landscape images in shaping the American spirit.[70] In the book-length poem, the Ojibway Hiawatha takes Minnehaha, the daughter of a Dacotah arrow maker, as his bride. She derives her name from the laughing water of the creek and its small picturesque falls, which had been much depicted after the poem's publication (fig. 15). Sympathetic with the iconic power of the natural landscape around the falls, Cleveland hoped to communicate its richness through the organic design of what was then the region's largest park.

Minnehaha Falls had become a pilgrimage site by the 1870s

"Where the Falls of Minnehaha
Flash and gleam among the oak trees
Laugh and leap into the valley."
(From Longfellow's Poem "Hiawatha")

FIGURE 15. Early twentieth-century postcard of Minnehaha
Falls with words from Longfellow's *The Song of Hiawatha*.

as thousands of visitors, poem in hand, came to bask in its mist (fig. 16). At the same time that literary enthusiasts were enshrining the site, numerous entrepreneurs sought to tap the water power for milling and industrial use. When, after the Minneapolis park system had been under way for three or four years, an opportunity came to purchase the falls, Cleveland and other progressive Minnesotans moved to action.[71] In 1888, Cleveland delivered the Minneapolis Society of Fine Arts address, titled "The Aesthetic Development of the United Cities of St. Paul and Minneapolis." By fusing the issue of civic character to the conservation of "native" land-scape for public use, Cleveland's address set the stage for the next generation's progressive political modus operandi. He used the address to argue passionately for the preservation of the falls and to educate his audience about the potential for a city intimately connected to its natural structure:

> I would have the city itself such a work of art as it may be the fitting abode of a race of men and women whose lives are devoted to a nobler end than money-getting, and whose efforts shall be inspired and sustained by the grandeur and beauty of the scenes in which their lives are passed. Nature offers us such advantages as no other city could rival and such as if properly developed would exhibit the highest attainment of art in appropriating the natural elements on which all art is founded.[72]

At Minnehaha all of the themes carefully explored in *Landscape Architecture, as Applied to the Wants of the West* were brought to fruition. Minnehaha Park served two important purposes: at one level it largely completed Cleveland's park system by link-ing the southern extent of the system hydrologically and recre-ationally to the Mississippi River (fig. 17); and as an individual park, the unembellished design, dotted with existing native flora, stood as a symbol of nature—the very nature under siege by the movement of civilization itself. When Minnehaha Creek was annexed to the city in the 1890s, the "Grand Rounds"—a term coined by Folwell—were completed. With this addition and the gradual development of the Mississippi River parkways came the realization of a city park system based on public access

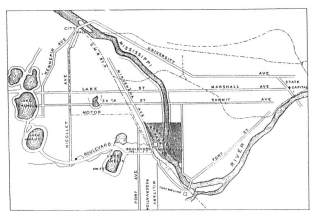

FIGURE 17. Location of proposed park, from *Aesthetic Development of the United Cities of St. Paul and Minneapolis* (1888).

to and control of major elements of its watershed, highly appropriate to a place whose name means "city of water."

There is evidence in addition to his preservation activism at Minnehaha Falls to suggest that by the early 1880s Cleveland believed that landscape conservation was within the realm of the new profession. He continued to write and lecture on forestry. An article on tree culture in the *Nation* was so well received that Charles Sprague Sargent and others encouraged Cleveland to publish *The Culture and Management of Our Native Forests* in 1882.[73]

One of his most enlightened suggestions on forest conservation concerned the wooded landscape surrounding Natural Bridge, Virginia. There, Cleveland recommended that a large forest reserve be set aside to serve "schools of practical instruction in forestry and arboriculture."[74] His argument that there was no nobler use of the property "than devoting it to the practical and illustrative instruction of forestry" came more than a decade before Olmsted and Gifford Pinchot's famous forestry efforts at Biltmore near Asheville, North Carolina. Though Cleveland's practice by the 1880s centered on grand urban initiatives, he also clearly identified a conservation ethic as an appropriate companion to landscape intervention.

Cleveland's productivity began to wane by the late 1880s and early 1890s. For a time he practiced with his son Ralph, who was briefly superintendent of Lakewood Cemetery in Minneapolis. The father-son partnership concentrated on parks and cemeteries, and they used the term "landscape gardeners" to describe their practice, perhaps alluding to a greater focus on planting design than in the past. They designed Madison (1891) and Riverview Parks (1893) in Quincy, Illinois, and Powderhorn Park (1892) in Minneapolis. One of the more lasting projects of the period was their design for the first campus of the University of Minnesota (1891–92), where academic buildings were sited along the edge of a parklike environment above a railroad gorge (fig. 18).[75]

Cleveland's writing during those years took on a retrospective, even a nostalgic, tone. In 1886, for example, he published *Voyages of a Merchant Navigator* about his father's seafaring adventures and resultant dignity of character.[76] *Social Life and Literature Fifty Years Ago,* published two years later, was both a commentary on the importance of literature in shaping his life philosophy and a critique of the eroded state of contemporary culture. In a letter to his friend Folwell, Cleveland criticized Edward Bellamy's influential book *Looking Backward, 2000–*

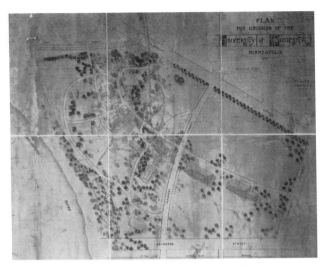

FIGURE 18. Plan for the grounds of the University of Minnesota, designed by H. W. S. Cleveland and Son, 1892. *University of Minnesota Archives.*

1887, noting a general deterioration of the values he held as the foundation for cultural order and stability.[77]

In the late 1890s, Cleveland moved to Hinsdale, Illinois, to live the rest of his life with Ralph, who became a photographer for architects of the Chicago School, including Daniel Burnham and Louis Sullivan. Charles Loring visited there in 1898, suggesting that Cleveland write a paper for the American Park and Outdoor Art Association meeting scheduled that year for Minneapolis. Cleveland's initial response to that request, "I have been dead too long for that," was likely as much a commentary on the changing world as concern for his advanced years.[78]

The world was changing indeed. Philosophically Cleveland

was very much a product of the first half of the nineteenth century. He held the conviction that an elite group with nobility of character was justly commissioned to set the course of civilization for the good of the nation. But by the 1890s American populism was growing in the western regions only recently broken by the plow, and with the turn of the twentieth century came the dawn of the Progressive Era.

In the wake of immigration, increased racial tension, and the expanding roles of women and minorities in society, some social theorists and practitioners pressed for a new participatory mode of action in public life. Cleveland's design perspective was carried forward with great enthusiasm by a new generation of designers. In the Midwest his work had a direct and also a subliminal influence on Prairie School landscape architects. O. C. Simonds, in particular, seems to have inherited and extended the Cleveland legacy (fig. 19).[79] Simonds's work followed on Cleveland's in Graceland Cemetery, where his use of native and common plants in new spatially evocative settings created a "prairie style." When Simonds arrived in 1878, he saw the simple, practical beauty of a country cemetery in the city. After Simonds became superintendent of the cemetery in 1881, the need to provide a planted structure for the increasing number and scale of the monuments gave birth to the conventionalized prairie concepts of the long and broad view.

Cleveland's legacy to Prairie School designers is perhaps most obvious in Highland Park, the community he designed in relation to a natural ravine landscape. (The ravine was among the eight Illinois landscape types listed by Wilhelm Miller in his

FIGURE 19. Willow walk, Tenney Park, Madison, Wisconsin, designed by O. C. Simonds, ca. 1902–7. *Photograph by Charles N. Brown, State Historical Society of Wisconsin.*

1915 publication *The Prairie Spirit in Landscape Gardening*). Important from a historiographic perspective is the fact that the ravines in and just south of Highland Park later became the inspiration for both O. C. Simonds and the best-known prairie-style designer, Jens Jensen, who had a studio there.

Cleveland's work was especially important to urban designers. In their foundation of the new profession of city planning in the first decade of the twentieth century, Frederick Law Olmsted Jr. and John Nolen embodied ideas articulated by Cleveland.[80] The architect Daniel Burnham, too, was profoundly affected both by the Parisian boulevard model and by the ideas of the connective park system as a basic formal structure of urban growth. Cleveland's projects were often depicted as models for civic improvement work. Minnehaha Creek, where he had designed a parkway along the water to link lakeside parks with Minnehaha Falls and the Mississippi River, was one of two midwestern projects depicted in Charles Mulford Robinson's book *Modern Civic Art or the City Made Beautiful* (1903). And Drexel Boulevard was depicted in the Minneapolis Plan (begun in 1909) completed by Burnham's successor, Edward Bennett.

These new urban designers considered many of Cleveland's ideas visionary. When Simonds gave an address at the American Park and Outdoor Art Association meeting (1898) on the development and influence of landscape architecture at the turn of the century, he captured the essence of Cleveland's work with the simple phrase, "he taught us how to make cities."[81] *Landscape Architecture, as Applied to the Wants of the West* is a glimpse into Cleveland's insights.

SUMMARY OF CHAPTERS

Cleveland begins his first chapter by reminding the reader of the wide-ranging effect of Downing's *Treatise on the Theory and Practice of Landscape Gardening*, a book offering "the first intimation of the existence of an art" focused on the arrangement of public and private grounds. Cleveland argues that landscape designers should concentrate on the "essential principles which lie at the foundation of the art." That task was especially important in the West where society had yet to attain the "condition of elaborate culture." Cleveland presents the residential example as a way of illustrating the importance of that preparatory work regardless of the scale. He concludes the first chapter by offering a definition for the profession: *"Landscape Gardening, or more properly Landscape Architecture, is the art of arranging land so as to adapt it most conveniently, economically and gracefully, to any of the varied wants of civilization."*

   In this chapter, then, Cleveland suggests that the art of landscape design should move beyond traditional landscape gardening to landscape architecture, a new profession capable of a larger scale and broader scope of practice. He also suggests that at its best landscape design might serve the core needs of American civilization. Cleveland argues that a focus on extraneous decoration only diverts attention from the important work of landscape architecture, the "essential principles" at the foundation of the art that spurn the blind application of embellishment in favor of a direct connection to the essential rightness of place. In discussing the importance of connecting to place, Cleveland reveals his commitment to an organic design principle (although he does not directly use the term).

In chapter 2, Cleveland concentrates more specifically on the role of landscape architecture in creating the framework of life on a private estate. As in chapter 1, he argues that the landscape architect should not simply serve to provide a tasteful decorative aspect to the landscape after the major decisions have been made, but rather should actively engage an array of complex problems related to making home landscapes. Because he saw the layout of a rural home in the unsettled West as being a primary expression of values that would last for generations, his first concern lay in those issues related to the siting and erection of a house, in its wider context, not in the design of gardens or in the inappropriate use of ornament. He foresaw that design should look forward to the time when the value of lands in the vicinity of such houses would be so great and growth so prevalent that the subdivision of the estate would be necessary. This creation of a framework for community order was for him the most significant charge to the landscape architect of a private estate in the West.

The organic approach is a cornerstone of the book. In presenting it in chapter 2, Cleveland fastens on the essential expressive qualities of the land. He defines the role of the landscape architect to interpret these qualities through design, not to destroy them or cover them with ornamental additions. He clarifies the danger: "Moreover it is by no means impossible that elaborate ornamentation should destroy or seriously detract from the general expression otherwise conveyed, as in the instance of conferring an air of ostentatious display upon an otherwise pleasant and attractive home, or detracting from the dignity of an imposing situation, by diverting attention from the sublime or beautiful natural features, which are sufficient in themselves to excite admiration and occupy attention."

Cleveland's apparent short-schrift treatment of the private estate as a conventional nineteenth-century landscape garden signaled his allegiance to the concerns of the new landscape architecture. He was most interested in the larger order of civic landscape typologies that had engaged his practice prior to the Civil War and, after the war, had propelled Olmsted and Vaux's practice to the front ranks of landscape design in the eastern United States. Cleveland clearly was banking on making this sort of practice in the West himself, and chapter 3 reveals his true aims as he began to understand Chicago's pivotal position in the region's destiny. Railroad building and related business developments provided practical opportunities for new patterns of urbanization and especially town and suburban design.

Cleveland discusses the "rapid conversion of wilderness to advanced cultivation" (a topic he develops in much greater detail later in the book) as a way of critiquing the design needs of the Midwest and Great Plains. Despite those rapid changes, he suggests there has been little progress in the art of arranging communities. He explores his idea of designed urbanization in several contexts, especially the organic aesthetic, which he expresses here as a plea for the preservation of natural topographic features of expressive interest.

Another context introduced in this chapter and developed in subsequent ones is the need for a connective system of public parklands and other open spaces. He discusses the idea in relation to Chicago where opportunities to create a seamless system had already been lost in the early development of the separate South, West, and Lincoln park districts in the 1860s. The center of Chicago was so densely developed on a grid of lots and streets that new parks planned for the edges would act as "orphanage appendages" until the city grew.

In chapter 4, Cleveland adds detail to his concept for connecting public open spaces by describing a system in a hypothetical city where the central business district, appropriately adorned, is connected by planted boulevards to outlying parks and suburban additions. Such a plan, Cleveland argues, provides unique spaces for the inhabitants of individual neighborhoods as well as designed linkages offering efficient and aesthetically pleasing circulation routes throughout the city. Here Cleveland mentions Paris as the premier European example of such a system. Cleveland again discusses Chicago to describe how opportunities for change are lost after an area is developed. Adding London and Boston to his case, he suggests that even a devastating fire does not ensure that boulevards and radial streets can be built. Private property rights will reign supreme and ultimately define the extent and connectedness of the public realm.

Much of this chapter is dedicated to a fuller development of Cleveland's organic perspective related to community design. Though such innovative design moves made sense even in relatively flat areas, the approach was especially important in places that exhibited significant topographic relief. He uses a discussion of natural ravines to suggest a better way of designing communities that are intimately tied to the existing landscape. Cleveland argues that those features have been typically separated from the community and suggests an approach that would make the important natural features accessible to the general public as integral elements of a community form.

In chapter 5, Cleveland explores the park as an essential component of his open-space system. He reemphasizes the importance of parks to the making of democratic cities as he argues the need for future-oriented planning and careful site selection. In this chapter he also lays out a related strategy whereby in the far-flung cities of the West, the bones of small decentralized parks could be established in a cost-effective phased approach. He argues, again, persuasively that topography is of primary importance and that new parks can be first graded and drained. Planting and structures could follow over time if these fundamentals were well executed. In this way, the character of a surrounding neighborhood could be developed in an organic manner commensurate with the program of the park, and the expenditures of changing a prior scheme would be avoided.

Cleveland's extended discussion of Parc Buttes Chaumont in the industrial northeast end of Paris, then just nine years old at the publication of his book, seems on the surface to be quite inconsistent with both the practicality of a phased approach and with the deeper streams of his organic aesthetic. Yet it did correspond with his practical sense of the need to build parks of intermediate scale in all sorts of districts and neighborhoods so that the values of the park could accrue to the inhabitants of its surrounds.

It is in chapter 6 that Cleveland fully addresses the crisis of change alluded to earlier as the principal argument for implementing his approach to design and planning. Chicago, he points out, was only the focal point of a large hinterland landscape filled with resources. The rapidly increasing intensity of settlement and development meant that action should be taken quickly before opportunities to form the landscape were lost forever. Cleveland apparently believed that the new profession was responsible for planning that large region. While he suggests forest planting at the grandest of scales to improve the climate (a perspective more fully developed in the concluding essay), his principal concern here is still in the creation of a spatial structure for advancing civilization. At the heart of this argument is, again, the need for a formal civil framework upon which could develop the rapid creation of culture in the western United States. Cleveland asserts, finally, that the civilizing authority to guide those significant changes was not only the responsibility of landscape architecture, but also of all men of taste and learning who would hire landscape architects to bring forth civil values in the physical, topographic bones of the new communities that would define America.

In the forest planting essay Cleveland demonstrates his understanding of forest culture theory and debate. He quotes from a number of leading forestry experts and discusses the establishment of Arbor Day in Nebraska and "congressional action," probably referring to the Timber Culture Act of 1873. Cleveland suggests that the accelerated pace of forest destruction justifies a massive tree-planting effort on the Great Plains to provide timber for home and railroad, encourage intelligent settlement, and ameliorate the climate. In discussing a forestry crisis, he quotes his old friend George Barrell Emerson's 1846 book *Report on the Trees and Shrubs Growing Naturally in the Forests of Massachusetts*. The crisis that Emerson had suggested years earlier must have seemed imminent by the early 1870s as civilization prepared to move into a huge, largely treeless portion of American geography.

Cleveland argues that if trees were planted in sufficient quantities, the new forest cover would ameliorate the climate, bringing a barren landscape to life. He includes a number of quotations from George Perkins Marsh's *Man and Nature* (1864) in support of his assertion that an extensive forestry effort would create a much wetter and cooler place. Cleveland further argues that large-scale tree planting is best implemented by the railroads. To make that case he includes information on a railroad tree-planting experiment conducted by R. S. Elliott of the Kansas Pacific Railway. Cleveland suggests that the railroad industry could establish nurseries along the rails as Elliott had done, providing a source of trees for construction and settlement, and that forestry efforts be managed by reputable tree-planting professionals. The result of such large-scale planting would be the "conversion of an uninhabitable desert into a region of agricultural wealth capable of supporting a dense population."

NOTES

Research for this introduction was funded in part by the Institute for the Arts and Humanistic Studies and the Center for Studies in Landscape History at The Pennsylvania State University and the

Design Center for the American Urban Landscape and the Graduate School of the University of Minnesota.

¹ H. W. S. Cleveland, *Landscape Architecture, as Applied to the Wants
of the West; with an Essay on Forest Planting on the Great Plains* (Chicago:
Jansen, McClurg & Co., 1873), 17, hereafter cited as Cleveland, *LAAWW*.
The major portion of the book was republished as H. W. S. Cleveland,
Landscape Architecture, as Applied to the Wants of the West, ed. Roy Lubove
(Pittsburgh: University of Pittsburgh Press, 1965), hereafter cited as
Lubove, *LAAWW*. Lubove did not include the "Essay on Forest
Planting" and made "minor alterations in spelling and punctuation
reflecting practices no longer current." Scholarly attention to Cleveland
has been thin over the years. The first piece to recognize his importance
to the development of the profession was Theodora Kimball Hubbard,
"H. W. S. Cleveland: An American Pioneer in Landscape Architecture
and City Planning," *Landscape Architecture* 20 (January 1930): 92–111.
Succeeding works include Karl Haglund, "Rural Tastes, Rectangular
Ideas, and the Skirmishes of H. W. S. Cleveland," *Landscape Architecture*
66 (January 1976); Eleanor M. McPeck, "Horace W. S. Cleveland in the
East, 1854–1878," unpublished paper, Harvard University, 1972; Virginia
Luckhardt, "Horace William Shaler Cleveland: An Overview of the Life
and Work of an Early American Landscape Architect," unpublished
masters thesis, University of Wisconsin, 1983; and Nancy J. Volkman,
"Landscape Architecture on the Prairie: The Work of H. W. S.
Cleveland," *Kansas History* 10 (Spring 1987): 89–110. Our understanding
of Cleveland presented in this introduction is built on a base provided by
William H. Tishler's thirty years of research. His published works
include William H. Tishler and Virginia Luckhardt, "H. W. S.
Cleveland: Pioneer Landscape Architect to the Upper Midwest,"
Minnesota History 49 (Fall 1985): 281–91, and "Horace Cleveland: The
Chicago Years," in *Midwestern Landscape Architecture*, ed. William H.
Tishler (Urbana: University of Illinois Press in cooperation with Library
of American Landscape History, 2000), 25–40.

² Cleveland was not alone; during the same period Frederick Law
Olmsted was quite uncertain about the future of the profession. The
years before Olmsted's move to Boston were especially unpredictable

times for him. Biographers discuss his poor mental outlook as various employment opportunities were lost. See the classic Laura Wood Roper, *FLO: A Biography of Frederick Law Olmsted* (Baltimore: Johns Hopkins University Press, 1973), 360–62, and Witold Rybczynski, *A Clearing in the Distance: Frederick Law Olmsted and America in the Nineteenth Century* (New York: Simon & Schuster, 1999), 335–37.

[3] Cleveland, *LAAWW*, 95–147.

[4] Various factors contribute to an overemphasis on Olmsted's influence. For one thing, some of the historiography that elevates Olmsted to hero status inevitably diminishes the importance of other landscape architects of the era. Also, the fact that Cleveland worked for (or at least with) Olmsted briefly in the late 1860s might seem to imply Olmsted's role as mentor. And the tone of Cleveland's letters to Olmsted suggests a humble respect, though that respectful tone, found in much of Cleveland's correspondence, likely communicates more about his character and demeanor than the character of his relationship with Olmsted.

[5] Ruskin's influence on Olmsted is developed in Irving D. Fisher, *Frederick Law Olmsted and the City Planning Movement in the United States* (Ann Arbor, Mich.: UMI Research Press, 1986), 21–22, 49–50, 75–81. For a discussion of Cleveland's aesthetic foundations, see Daniel Joseph Nadenicek, "Emerson's Aesthetic and Natural Design: A Theoretical Foundation for the Work of Horace William Shaler Cleveland," in *Nature and Ideology,* ed. Joachim Wolschke-Bulmahn (Washington, D.C.: Dumbarton Oaks, 1997), 59–80.

[6] Cleveland, *LAAWW*, 17.

[7] Cleveland's father recorded his seafaring experiences in Richard Jeffry Cleveland, *Voyages and Commercial Enterprises of the Sons of New England* (New York: Leavitt and Allen, 1855) and Horace Cleveland's own compilation of his father's writings is *Voyages of a Merchant Navigator of the Days That Are Past* (New York: Harper & Brothers, 1886). Richard Cleveland's exploits are also mentioned in Samuel Eliot Morison, *The Maritime History of Massachusetts, 1783–1860* (Boston: Houghton Mifflin, 1921), 60, 73.

[8] The pervasiveness of the rural ideal is discussed in Tamara Plakins Thornton, *Cultivating Gentlemen: The Meaning of Country Life among the Boston Elite, 1765–1860* (New Haven: Yale University Press, 1989).

⁹ This Unitarian perspective on human improvement and its influence on Cleveland's life and career are more fully developed in Daniel Joseph Nadenicek, "The Other Side of Progress: Cleveland, Longfellow, and the Superintendents of Society," *Nature and Technology: Selected CELA Annual Conference Papers* (Ames, Iowa: Council of Educators in Landscape Architecture, 1995), 97–108.

¹⁰ Elizabeth Palmer Peabody was another lifelong contact of the Cleveland family. She was a teacher at a Lancaster school for girls also managed in part by Dorcas Cleveland. Peabody was one of the originators of the active learning approach adopted in American kindergarten education and the sister of Sophia (who married Nathaniel Hawthorne) and Mary (who married Horace Mann). The relationship of the Clevelands to the Peabodys is recounted in Lousie Hall Tharp, *The Peabody Sisters of Salem* (Boston: Little, Brown, 1950), 24–25, 45, 158.

¹¹ Many New Englanders considered tropical environments salubrious; see Nathaniel Parker Willis, *Health Trip to the Tropics* (New York: Charles Scribner, 1853). The Clevelands in their official capacity in Cuba arranged trips for Sophia Peabody and Ralph Waldo Emerson's brother among others. Horace Cleveland's brother Henry spent the last months of his life attempting to convalesce (probably from tuberculosis) in Cuba; see Henry R. Cleveland, *Selection from the Writings of Henry R. Cleveland*, ed. George S. Hillard (Boston: Freeman and Bolles, 1844).

¹² In Richard Overton, *The Burlington Route: A History of the Burlington Lines* (New York: Knopf, 1965), is a map that shows the Burlington running through Prophetstown, Illinois. Cleveland recalled the experience of the town in the 1830s in four letters to William Merchant Richardson French, who himself was there, on a bridge building project, apparently, September 19, 21, 22, and 26, 1871. Cleveland's brother, Richard Cleveland, was an engineer who lived in Iowa, but made railroad surveys in Illinois in about 1837 and 1838, the same period of Cleveland's early trips. Richard married Elizabeth Hiller Seeley of Prophetstown. This marriage and the Seeley family are mentioned in Cleveland to French, 19 September 1871. Also, Cleveland writes two days later, "It seems very odd to me to think of Prophetstown as being within the influence of the railroad." Cleveland to French, 21 September 1871.

¹³ Horace Cleveland to Blanche Willis Howard, undated (ca. 1891), Northwest Architectural Archives, University of Minnesota. One of a group of 1891–93 letters to Howard recently acquired.

¹⁴ Cleveland later recounted the significance of meeting with that group and of other important literary encounters in *Social Life and Literature Fifty Years Ago* (Boston: Cupples and Hurd, 1888). The close relationship of members of the Five of Clubs is also shown in Henry Cleveland, *Selection from Writings.*

¹⁵ In one letter Horace told the poet that his passages "kindle a glow of grateful feeling . . . [and] come home to me like the echo of the surging of my own heart." Horace Cleveland to Henry Wadsworth Longfellow, 13 February 1881, Longfellow Papers, Houghton Library, Harvard.

¹⁶ Cleveland quoted the following: "Look not mournfully into the past. It comes not back again. Wisely improve the present. It is thine. Go forth and meet the shadowy future, without fear and with a manly heart." Horace Cleveland to Henry Wadsworth Longfellow, 5 February 1881, Longfellow Papers, Houghton Library, Harvard.

¹⁷ The Boston elite had engaged in agricultural pursuits as means of elevating rural citizens for a long time, and by the time of Cleveland and Copeland's involvement in the endeavor, scientific farming had added a professional focus to the avocation. For discussions of the practice, see Thornton, *Cultivating Gentlemen*, 204–5, as well as Donald B. Marti, *To Improve the Soil and the Mind: Agricultural Societies, Journals, and Schools in the Northeastern States, 1791–1865* (Ann Arbor, Mich.: University Microfilms International, 1979), 209–13.

¹⁸ Cleveland believed, as his future partner Robert Morris Copeland later wrote, that a managed rural landscape offered everything that might "expand the mind and ennoble the soul." Robert Morris Copeland, *Country Life: A Handbook of Agriculture, Horticulture, and Landscape Gardening* (Boston: John P. Jewett, 1859), ii.

¹⁹ An early Cleveland and Copeland advertisement highlighting services in "agricultural engineering" demonstrates the importance of agricultural work in the first years of their practice.

²⁰ The state farm at Westborough was a reform school. Cleveland and Copeland designed the landscape in keeping with the belief that engagement with the landscape would cultivate young minds. George Emerson

had written his *Report on the Trees and Shrubs Growing Naturally in the Forests of Massachusetts* (Boston: Dutton and Wentworth, 1846) to the Massachusetts Legislature, and his forest studies and experiments were ahead of their time. (As a consequence of his interest in the subject he was instrumental in founding the Arnold Arboretum in 1872.) When Cleveland and Copeland began their practice, Emerson retained the designers to help with tree-planting efforts at his estate on Chelsea Harbor. There Cleveland, Copeland, and Emerson planted numerous European and North American tree species, monitoring the adaptability of each to the sandy loam and windswept conditions of the site. See Ida Hay, "George Barrell Emerson and the Establishment of the Arnold Arboretum," *Arnoldia* 54 (1994): 17.

[21] Emerson's *Nature*, first published in 1836, became a seminal text for American transcendentalist philosophy. Pushing beyond Unitarian philosophy, Emerson uncoupled the shackles of organized religion, advocating a connection to the "oversoul" through a neo-Platonic interaction with the elements of nature. Cleveland betrayed his affinity for Emerson in publications and correspondence on numerous occasions throughout his life.

[22] Emerson developed his aesthetic theories in his first essay, "Art." Ralph Waldo Emerson, *The Complete Works of Ralph Waldo Emerson*, ed. Edward W. Emerson, vol. 2 (Boston: Houghton Mifflin, 1903–4), and "Thoughts on Art," in *Complete Works*, vol. 7. Those ideas are also discussed in Nadenicek, "Emerson's Aesthetic."

[23] Nadenicek, "Emerson's Aesthetic," 68–71.

[24] H. W. S. Cleveland, "Landscape Gardening," *Christian Examiner* 43 (May 1855): 384–401.

[25] Robert Morris Copeland and H. W. S. Cleveland, *A Few Words on the Central Park* (Boston: n.p., 1856), 4. Emerson used similar language to describe the design intent at Sleepy Hollow; see "Address to the Inhabitants of Concord at the Consecration of Sleepy Hollow," Emerson Papers, Houghton Library, Harvard. Also see Daniel Joseph Nadenicek, "Sleepy Hollow Cemetery: Transcendental Garden and Community Park," *Journal of the New England Garden History Society* 3 (Fall 1993): 11–12. Cleveland continued to write of his distaste for the inappropriate use of artificial embellishment in numerous publications. He discusses the problem at length in *LAAWW*.

[26] Emerson, "Consecration Address."

[27] Ibid. Emerson was also pleased that the site had not been "deformed by bad art," the art of superfluous decoration, but rather highlighted "the native and hidden graces of the landscape."

[28] One famous example is Olmsted's incorporation of tropical effects in Central Park.

[29] It was also uncharted territory because even Emerson and Greenough were unaware of how the organic principle might directly inspire particular works of art.

[30] "What work of man will compare with the plantation of a park? It dignifies life . . . I do not wonder that they [parks] are the chosen badge and point of pride of the European nobility. But how much more are they needed by us, anxious, over driven Americans, to stanch and appease the fury of temperament which our climate bestows." The park at Sleepy Hollow also included an arboretum "so that every child may be shown growing, side by side, the eleven oaks of Massachusetts." Emerson, "Consecration Address." See also Nadenicek, "Sleepy Hollow," 13.

[31] Emerson wrote that Sleepy Hollow "fortunately lies adjoining the Agricultural Society's ground, to the New Burial Ground, to the Court House and Town House, making together a large block of public ground, permanent property of town and country—all of the ornaments of either adding so much value to all."

[32] The fact that the Concord community had for several years under John Keyes's leadership considered the interrelationship of all public spaces no doubt influenced this innovative thinking by the mid-1850s. In addition, it was common practice among the Concord literati to take a daily walk—to wend their way from the town to the fields and forests of the countryside. Emerson, too, practiced the ritual almost daily. The connection of open spaces facilitated the practice of engaging nature.

[33] The idea linking public spaces conceived in Concord quickly evolved and was applied to an urban context. Cleveland and Copeland's suggestions were welcomed because the Back Bay had been incrementally filled for several years, by 1856 creating a new landscape in need of design. Perhaps in response to their suggestions, the committee that was designated to consider the future use of the new in-fill landscape wrote in 1856: "It is believed that an ornamental avenue of this character . . . with stately dwelling-houses on each side, connecting the public parks in the centre of a busy city with attractive and quiet, although populous

country is a thing not possible of construction elsewhere in the world; and those places where some thing of the same kind already exists have been rendered famous in the consequence." *Report of the Committee Appointed under the Resolves of 1856, Chap. 76, in Relation to Lands in the Back Bay* (Boston: Senate No. 17, 1857), 14–15. On Cleveland and Copeland's suggestions, see also Walter Muir Whitehall, *Boston: A Topographic History* (Cambridge: Belknap Press, 1968), 151.

[34] Cleveland to Howard (ca. 1891). While we know only a little of Cleveland's life during the Civil War, the Howard letters suggest that considerable energy was given to rifle clubs. Cleveland was also involved in arms research and perhaps sales. He wrote widely on the topic; see H. W. S. Cleveland, "Rifle-Clubs," *Atlantic Monthly* 10 (Sept. 1862): 303–10.

[35] Near the close of the Civil War he wrote *Hints to Riflemen* (New York: D. Appleton, 1864) and after the war served as an agent for the Massachusetts Arms Company. Cleveland may have worked for Olmsted's firm or Olmsted may have helped him secure a position in direct employ of the park.

[36] Cleveland engaged in an ongoing correspondence with Olmsted in the succeeding years. And Olmsted appears to have used his influence to help Cleveland secure work at various times.

[37] Horace's brother had married Sarah Perkins. James Perkins was a brother of the more famous Thomas Handasyd Perkins. These family and business connections were built together, as it was Forbes and Perkins family practice to hire relatives and friends of relatives. That was the policy that brought nephew John Murray Forbes into the Perkins counting house and sent him around the Horn to China as a young man. Later, Charles Russell Lowell, the son of poet James Russell Lowell, would become Forbes's protégé. Following upon Henry Cleveland's marriage to Sarah this practice devolved to Horace's own son, Ralph, who worked on the Burlington line in Iowa. For a discussion of Perkins and Forbes's seafaring activities, see Morison, *Maritime History.* And for the railroad efforts of the Boston elite, see Arthur M. Johnson and Barry E. Supple, *Boston Capitalists and Western Railroads: A Study in the Nineteenth-Century Railroad Investment Process* (Cambridge: Harvard University Press, 1967), 14–286. Charles Perkins, cousin of Cleveland's sister-in-law Sarah Perkins, first served as Superintendent of Western Operations for the CB&Q. Ralph Cleveland's visits to Apple Trees, the

Burlington, Iowa, home of Charles Perkins, is noted in one of the several privately printed volumes: see Charles Elliot Perkins, *Family Letters and Reminiscences, 1865–1907*, ed. Edith Forbes Cunningham (Portland, Me.: Anthoensen Press, 1949).

³⁸ The Hinsdale design was also featured with Olmsted and Vaux's Riverside design in CB&Q promotions of suburbs along its lines, "Suburbs of the Chicago, Burlington and Quincy Railroad Illustrated," an advertisement pamphlet of the CB&Q, 1875, Chicago Historical Society. The cover bears an inscription from Emerson. Inside is a page-length essay on suburban homes. The designers of both Riverside and the Robbins Addition in Hinsdale are prominently mentioned. The Cleveland-French correspondence also specifically mentions potential arrangements with Charles Perkins to provide drafting (Cleveland to French, 22 January 1871, Pusey Library, Harvard) and a payment of $500 from the Burlington and Missouri River Railroad with a note from Perkins (Cleveland to French, 3 October 1871). See also western cemetery commissions listed in *A Few Words on the Arrangement of Rural Cemeteries* (Chicago: George K. Hazlitt, 1881), which mentions work in Junction City, Kansas, for example.

³⁹ By the 1880s it was estimated that the railroads depleted American forests at the rate of 300,000 acres per year. See M. G. Kern, *The Relation of Railroads to Forest Supplies and Forestry*, USDA, Forestry Division Bulletin no. 1 (Washington D.C.: GPO, 1887).

⁴⁰ Cleveland, *LAAWW*, 34–36, and Lubove, *LAAWW*, xii–xxi.

⁴¹ H. W. S. Cleveland, "The Grand Traverse Region of Michigan," *Atlantic Monthly* 26 (Aug. 1870): 191.

⁴² Often nineteenth-century partnerships were looser arrangements than today. Cleveland and French seemed to collaborate directly on certain projects and work independently on others.

⁴³ The essays were bound together with numerous testimonials from satisfied clients.

⁴⁴ A broadside advertisement for Boilvin's Addition to the town, n.d., ca. 1875, Chicago Historical Society. Similar language with a direct association to the ravines can be found in "Highland Park" in Everett Chamberlain, *Chicago and Its Suburbs* (Chicago: T.A. Hungerford, 1874), 393.

⁴⁵ In Cleveland's correspondence with French, Frank Hawkins, the local superintendent of construction, was mentioned as prevailing upon

the partners to draft the plan in order to market the town by 1874. The let-ter reveals that the lots and streets were staked in the field before they were drawn. The printed plan of Highland Park is dated 1874, but correspon-dence from Cleveland to French, 22 September 1871, states that he (Cleve-land) "spent the day at Highland Park yesterday staking out avenues and paths. Mrs. P was disappointed that her husband did not have a regular plan and is quite intent on having it done." Cleveland-French Correspon-dence, Pusey Library, Harvard (Gift of Prentiss French).

[46] It can be argued that with this design, Cleveland and French estab-lished themselves as the first significant prairie landscape architects. The roots of the prairie mythos lie in the region's merging cultural and land-scape identity in the twenty-five-year period after the Civil War. The design of Highland Park and the nearby landscapes of the Lake Michigan shore around their ravines were among these deeply planted origins. Lance M. Neckar, "Fast-tracking Culture and Landscape: Horace William Shaler Cleveland and the Garden in the Midwest," in *Regional Garden Design in the United States,* ed. Therese O'Malley and Marc Treib (Washington D.C.: Dumbarton Oaks, 1995), 77–97.

[47] Copeland's brother-in-law, Charles F. Dunbar, was the editor of the *Boston Daily Advertiser* during those years. In the late 1860s Copeland used that publication as a soapbox from which to proclaim the wisdom of a network of connected spaces as opposed to a single centralized park.

[48] H. W. S. Cleveland, *The Public Grounds of Chicago: How to Give Them Character and Expression* (Chicago: Charles D. Lakely, 1869).

[49] Though at the time very much in the formative stage, Copeland's scheme included a number of spaces that were later incorporated into Boston's Emerald Necklace and Charles Eliot's regional plan. Robert Morris Copeland, *The Most Beautiful City in America: Essay and Plan for the Improvement of the City of Boston* (Boston: Lee & Shepard, 1872). Cleveland, *LAAWW*, 63.

[50] Arguably the publication of Robinson's book was very important to this vein of work and also seems directly related to Olmsted and Vaux's post–Civil War thinking. The most celebrated roadway of the period, Avenue L'Imperatrice, was a clear inspiration for that firm's designs of Brooklyn's "park way" boulevards.

[51] Cleveland wrote, "The burning of Chicago is simply the destruc-tion of the depot of the railroads which concentrate there, and the means

at command for her reconstruction are the combined wealth of the regions traversed by those roads. The energy and enterprise with which she is again springing up from her ashes, is based upon such knowledge of the value of those resources." Cleveland, *LAAWW*, 74.

⁵² Horace Cleveland to Frederick Law Olmsted, 19 December 1871, Olmsted Papers, Library of Congress. Cleveland helped position himself for such an opportunity through his publications, including articles on the importance of western tree-planting efforts for the *Railroad Gazette* and *Forest Planting.*

⁵³ The Timber Culture Act of 1873 offered 160 additional acres to settlers who engaged in substantial tree-planting efforts.

⁵⁴ Cleveland's book is also an indicator of his close association with prominent community leaders. Among his network of friends, clients, and business connections in Chicago included a centrally important group of three men, Governor William Bross, who was a friend of Thomas Barbour Bryan, and Bryan's nephew, Bryan Lathrop. Bryan and Lathrop were influential in the development of Graceland Cemetery. Bross (1813–1890) was perhaps the key figure in this network in the context of the publication of the book. A graduate of Williams College, he came to Chicago originally as a journalist for the *Prairie Herald*, and later for the *Democratic Press,* merged with the *Chicago Tribune.* Bross wrote three early essays (1854) in support of railroads for Chicago. He was a well-known leader in improvement circles, and an enthusiast for western development who in 1865 made an overland trip to California and in 1866 had addressed the New York Chamber of Commerce on the resources of the Far West and the Pacific Railroad. Prominently identified with the Mechanics Institute, he was also vice president and, later, president of the Chicago Academy of Sciences. He was nicknamed "Deacon Bross" because of his prominent connection to Presbyterianism. Bross was also, in 1875–6, the president of the botanical garden that Cleveland had designed for the South Parks (perhaps for Gage Park). Bross's wife, Mary Jane Jansen, was the sister of E. L. Jansen, a principal of the publishing firm, Jansen, McClurg & Co., who originally published *Landscape Architecture, as Applied to the Wants of the West.*

⁵⁵ Cleveland, *LAAWW*, 7.

⁵⁶ "Year by year the advancing tide of civilization is forcing its way by new routes into this region of mystery and beauty. Year by year new

lands are appropriated and the work of preparation for human habitation commenced, and year by year the sites are selected on which new towns and cities are to grow up and form the central points of supply and distribution of the regions around, which will teem with a dense population." Cleveland, *LAAWW*, 77.

[57] Cleveland's comparison of the city to a workshop is found in H. W. S. Cleveland, *The Aesthetic Development of the United Cities of St. Paul and Minneapolis* (Minneapolis: A. C. Bausman, 1888), 12. In *LAAWW*, 29, Cleveland wrote: "The vast regions yet lying undisturbed between the Mississippi and the Pacific comprise such resources of wealth and variety of sublime and picturesque features of natural scenery as can be seen on no other portion of the earth's surface, that is accessible to civilization. This is the raw material which is placed in our hands to be moulded to shape for the habitations of the nation, and such as we create, it must essentially remain for all future time."

[58] This is certainly one of the earliest published definitions of landscape architecture. Cleveland, *LAAWW*, 17.

[59] Ibid., 19.

[60] Roy Lubove's introduction emphasizes this plan for urban centers as the most significant contribution of Cleveland's book. Lubove, *LAAWW*, vii–xxi.

[61] At the same time Cleveland developed his idea of a connected park system in *LAAWW*, he laid out, with the help of his son Ralph, a new cemetery for his hometown of Lancaster, Massachusetts. The cemetery was designed somewhat like a city in that an ornamental center with numerous burial sites was connected by tree-lined drives to a forested edge, where only few graves were located here and there within a natural setting. See Daniel Nadenicek, "Eastwood Cemetery," unpublished paper, Council of Educators in Landscape Architecture, 1994, and Roberta Kessler, "Contemporary Issues in the Historic Landscape: Eastwood Cemetery in Lancaster, Massachusetts," unpublished master's thesis, Pennsylvania State University, 1995.

[62] Cleveland, *LAAWW*, 42–45. Although Cleveland certainly believed much could be done to enhance Chicago's future, certain mistakes such as the firmly entrenched city grid could not be easily changed.

[63] Cleveland was one of several residents who wrote personal statements in the aftermath of the Great Fire. He recollected that he carried everything from his office to the street below but that the congestion and

confusion prevented him from transporting the belongings to a safe location. Finally, convinced that the fire had turned in another direction, he returned everything to his office only to find the next day that the entire building had burned. H. W. S. Cleveland, manuscript dated 10 November 1871, Chicago Historical Society.

[64] The Northern Pacific Railroad, for example, halted all new construction for a number of years and put off tree-planting efforts until the early 1880s.

[65] M. G. Kern, *Relation of Railroads to Forestry*.

[66] H. W. S. Cleveland, *Suggestions for a System of Parks and Parkways for the City of Minneapolis* (Minneapolis: Johnson, Smith, & Harrison, 1883).

[67] Cleveland's introduction to the Minneapolis scene came through French's family relationship to George Leonard Chase, the fraternity brother and brother-in-law of Folwell. Cleveland and French were also introduced to civic leaders in both of the Twin Cities.

[68] Minneapolis was a successful flour-milling town on the St. Anthony Falls of the Mississippi River, and its principal progressive was Charles Loring. Loring was a driving force in the early development of the parks. Neckar, "Fast-tracking," 85–94.

[69] Ibid., 89–90. Olmsted later visited the park and observed Loring's and Cleveland's work. Because those efforts were completed prior to Olmsted's development of the Wooded Isle for the Worlds' Columbian Exposition it is possible that the use of native plants on the wild island in Minneapolis's Central Park influenced Olmsted's conception of the more famous design.

[70] Longfellow published *Hiawatha* at the time that Cleveland was beginning his transition from scientific agriculture to landscape design. One of the principal themes of the epic poem is the inevitable clash between the purity of landscape (of which the Native American was an integral part) and the progressive advance of civilization.

[71] A riverboat trip brought interested men and women to the site for a tour led by "Professor" Cleveland.

[72] Cleveland, *Aesthetic Development*, 13. For years the Minneapolis city parks used the motto "I would have the city itself . . . a work of art" in annual reports and promotional pieces.

[73] H. W. S. Cleveland, *The Culture and Management of Our Native Forests* (Springfield, Mass.: H. W. Rokker, 1882).

74 H. W. S. Cleveland, "The Natural Bridge," *The Debt Payer,* July 2, 1881.

75 A plan and statement about the design with the words "landscape gardeners" displayed are housed at the University of Minnesota archives. Later Daniel Chester French would be commissioned to design an exedra and cast a statue of the university's first president of the Board of Regents, John Sargent Pillsbury, an ensemble that now stands at the head of the knoll.

76 Of his father he wrote, "He had an ardent love of nature, and a keen perception of its attractive features, whether grandest or simplest forms. . . . He was an appreciative reader of the best literature of the day." These were values that Cleveland also upheld for a lifetime. H. W. S. Cleveland, *Voyages of a Merchant Navigator of the Days That Are Past* (New York: Harper & Brothers, 1886), 241.

77 H. W. S. Cleveland to William Watts Folwell, 14 May 1889, Minnesota Historical Society. While Cleveland's world view would not allow him to embrace Bellamy's ideas, the book was later one of the inspirations for Ebenezer Howard's garden city concept in *Tomorrow: A Real Path to Social Reform* (1898)

78 He later accepted the offer and wrote perhaps his last published piece, titled *The Influence of Parks on Children*.

79 An argument can also be made for Cleveland's influence on Charles Eliot and perhaps Warren Manning.

80 *Landscape Architecture, as Applied to the Wants of the West* was regularly included in important citations and bibliographies related to landscape architecture and planning. Robinson noted it in *Modern Civic Art: or the City Made Beautiful* (New York: G. P. Putnam, 1903). John Nolen included it in his citations in *Replanning Small Cities* (New York: B. W. Huebsch, 1912). Perhaps most important in the historiography of the profession, however, is its citation by Henry V. Hubbard and Theodora Kimball of Harvard in the first seminal text of professional education, *Introduction to the Study of Landscape Design* (New York: MacMillan, 1917), because more than forty years after its publication, it was still recommended as a general source for landscape architects.

81 O. C. Simonds, *Park and Cemetery* 8 (July 1898). The article included remarks made in Minneapolis at the meeting of the American Park and Outdoor Art Association. At this meeting Loring read Cleveland's paper *The Influence of Parks on the Character of Children*.

Landscape Architecture,
as Applied to the Wants of the West

LANDSCAPE ARCHITECTURE,

AS APPLIED TO THE

WANTS OF THE WEST;

WITH AN ESSAY ON

Forest Planting on the Great Plains.

BY H. W. S, CLEVELAND,

LANDSCAPE ARCHITECT.

CHICAGO:

JANSEN, McCLURG & CO.

1873.

PREFACE.

THE term "Landscape Architecture" is objectionable, as being only figuratively expressive of the art it is used to designate. I make use of it, under protest, as the readiest means of making myself understood, in the absence of a more appropriate term.

If the art is ever developed to the extent I believe to be within its legitimate limits, it will achieve for itself a name worthy of its position. Until it does so, it is idle to attempt to exalt it in the world's estimation, by giving it a high - sounding title. My object in these few pages is simply to show that, by whatever name it may be called, the subdivision and arrangement of land for the occupation of civilized men, is an art demanding the exercise of ingenuity, judgment and taste, and one which nearly concerns the interests of real estate proprietors, and the welfare and happiness of all future occupants.

A considerable portion of the " Essay on Forest Planting on the Great Plains," is made up from articles I have contributed from time to time to agricultural and scientific papers. All the correspondence, memoranda, etc., which I had collected on the subject for two years, during which I was engaged in its investigation, were destroyed in the great fire of October 9, 1871. The present essay has been prepared from recollection, with the aid of some of my previously published articles which had been preserved by friends, together with liberal quotations, bearing upon the subject, from reliable authors.

H. W. S. CLEVELAND.

CHICAGO, *Jan.*, 1873.

CONTENTS.

LANDSCAPE ARCHITECTURE.

CHAPTER I.

H E appearance of Downing's "Landscape Gardening," about thirty-five years ago, conveyed
to a large portion of the American public the
first intimation of the existence of an art, having distinct
principles and laws of its own, and dealing solely with
the problems involved in the tasteful arrangement of
public or private grounds.

Before the introduction of railroads, the luxury of a
country residence for men engaged in active business in
the city, was necessarily confined to so small a portion of
the population, that no general interest was felt in the
subject of the arrangement of grounds, and the demand
for the services of an educated landscape gardener was
too limited to warrant the adoption of the profession as a
means of support. With the facilities of locomotion
afforded by steam transport, came the demand for the
luxury of a rural home, and every city began sending
out suburban colonies along the lines thus rendered
accessible.

The new colonists had, however, for the most part, little knowledge of country life, and no conception even of the existence of governing principles for the arrangement of grounds, the grouping of trees to secure tasteful effects of shape and color, or the artistic development of naturally beautiful or picturesque features to attain a realization of the landscape painter's dreams.

To the large class who found themselves thus situated, delighted to escape from the restraints and the turmoil and dirt of the city, and eager to secure the utmost possible enjoyment from the new sources thus opened to them, yet feeling continually oppressed with the sense of their own ignorance and inexperience, Downing's book came like a new revelation, and attained at once a degree of success which was due alike to the admirable character of the work itself and to the fact of its appearing just in time to meet a great popular want.

Nothing like it had previously appeared in this country, and so few persons had any knowledge of foreign works on the subject, that his skillful adaptation of the principles of the art to our means, necessities and opportunities, had all the zest and freshness of original matter.

Since then the demand and supply have gone on annually increasing, till city and country have become so merged that it is hard to say where one ends and the other begins. The radius of available territory for suburban homes has extended with the opening of new roads, branches and lines of horse cars. Companies have made a lucrative business of buying attractive sites of comparatively wild land and arranging them tastefully

as suburban additions, finding ready sales for lots at prices which pay a fair profit on the cost of improvement. Everywhere the demand has proved how readily the popular heart responds to the opportunity, and the revolution which has been effected in the condition of the country surrounding every large city affords sufficient evidence of the innate love of nature, and the longing to secure the enjoyment of her attractions, which pervades the popular heart.

As a natural consequence, books and treatises upon landscape gardening and rural art, have multiplied till they have became an important branch of literature. Volumes and pamphlets of all sorts and sizes; original works, compilations, republications, and essays in the pages of horticultural journals have flowed from the press, till it would seem that no farther elucidation of the subject was required, or could be conveyed through the medium of publication; yet after twenty years experience as a professional landscape gardener, I am continually impressed with the inadequate conception of the scope of the art, which generally prevails, and I am convinced that the popular writers on the subject are largely responsible for the general ignorance. Not that they have failed to explain lucidly, and often in charming style, the esthetic principles of the art, and the management of the almost endless variety of combinations of natural and artificial decorations, whose tasteful introduction may often add very essentially to the beauty and interest of a country home; but that they have confined themselves so exclusively to such details that the idea has became almost universal that landscape gardening is solely a decorative art, the duties of which are comprised in the grouping of trees to secure the best effects of form and color, the disposition of wood, lawn and water, to form an artistic landscape, and the arrangement of all the details of ornament, such as flower beds, shrubbery, rustic work, fountains, waterfalls, etc., for the purpose of rendering the place attractive.

The evidences of this are continually brought home to me in the practice of my profession.

A man calls upon me for advice in regard to the arrangement of his grounds, and tells me he has built his house and made various improvements by grading and clearing, and now wants me to tell him how to finish it off. On visiting his place I find, perhaps, that he has placed his house in a position which may subject him to inconveniences which had never occurred to him, or that he might have secured advantages by placing it elsewhere which are impossible where it is. He has expended a large sum in grubbing up what he calls underbrush, and has thus destroyed the beauty of a natural wood, which now consists only of a collection of gaunt, naked looking stems of trees with mere tufts of foliage on their tops, which by no possibility can ever be made attractive either as individuals or groups. Elsewhere he has attempted to improve the grade by cutting down a hill which marred the even slope of the ground, but has succeeded only in giving it a formal look of cheerless discomfort. This he perceives, but instead of suspecting that it may be the result of his own mistakes, he only imagines it to be for the want of what remains to be done, which he expects me to direct. In other words, after destroying the natural beauty of the place, he looks to me to make it attractive by the introduction of artificial decorations, and not unfrequently he proceeds to give me directions as to the kind of ornaments he would like, and where and how they are to be bestowed; a fountain garishly displayed for the admiration of every wayfarer on the street; a rustic arbor or seat, not where any one would ever be tempted to make use of it, but where it may most conspicuously proclaim that this is the abode of rural felicity; flower beds, rock-work, serpentine walks, all to be arranged with the same obvious purpose of display; the idea throughout being that the place must be dressed up to look pretty, that the landscape gardener's duty is simply to arrange the dressing, and the test of his skill consists in making the most elaborate display of such baby-house furniture as the owner is willing to pay for. The proportion of those who have applied to me to arrange their grounds from the outset, fixing the positions of the buildings, and adapting the various subdivisions to the natural features of the place, so as to secure the utmost convenience, with the best possible development of graceful or picturesque effect, is insignificant in comparison with those who have sent for me after all these essential characteristics had been established beyond recall, and desired me to give the finishing touches which were to confer the crowning charm of attractive interest.

That writers on landscape gardening in this country have heretofore failed to give prominence to the really essential principles which lie at the foundation of the art, may be accounted for by the fact that they have supposed themselves to be addressing a class of readers inhabiting districts already brought to a condition of elaborate culture, and who would therefore be mainly interested in details of decoration. It is obvious that the new regions of the West require a vast amount of preliminary preparation before much attention can be paid to mere extraneous ornament. My object is to show not only that this preparatory work is justly the province of the landscape gardener, but that it is in reality the essentially important part of his art which gives character and expression to the whole, independently of mere decorations, which may or may not be in good taste, according as they correspond with the expression thus conferred. Yet the idea so generally prevails that the landscape gardener has no concern with these preliminary works, that I was repeatedly told when I first thought of establishing myself in the West, that I need not hope to succeed; that people were too much occupied in the great work of developing the resources of a new country to have time or means to devote to artistic display, and that the most I could hope for would be an occasional call to lay out some rich man's garden near the city, and for that I should probably be indebted to the ladies of the family.

Perceiving that these opinions were based upon an entire misconception of the scope of the art, whose principles I conceived to lie at the foundation of all improvements of land, my first efforts were directed to making known through the public press, and otherwise, as opportunity offered, the true definition of the term, which may be expressed in a condensed form as follows :

Landscape Gardening, or more properly Landscape Architecture, is the art of arranging land so as to adapt it most. conveniently, economically and gracefully, to any of the varied wants of civilization.

For whatever success I have met with in securing employment since coming to the West (which I gratefully acknowledge to have been far beyond my expectations), I feel that I have been mainly indebted to the persistent urging of this truth, and the conviction it has carried to the minds of those interested in the great real estate operations of the West, that it is the original design of arrangement which confers upon any place its intrinsic expression or character of beauty or picturesqueness, the want of which cannot be atoned for by any amount of subsequent dressing or decoration.

My object in the following pages is to prove the truth of the above definition by familiar illustrations, and set forth the extent and importance of its application to the wants of the West. I am not aware that any writer has ever attempted to apply the principles of the art, on the scale which I believe to be required to meet the demands which devolve upon us, yet I am confident that no one will deny that it involves issues of vital moment to the future of our country which deserve timely consideration.

CHAPTER II.

N order to make my meaning clear, I propose first to show what constitutes landscape architecture in the arrangement of a private estate, and then to illustrate the application of the same principles to larger areas.

Inexperienced persons continually deceive themselves with the idea that no art is required in the arrangement of ground for the ordinary purposes of domestic use as a family residence, beyond the exercise of intuitive skill and ingenuity, and almost every man imagines, till he tries, that he can do it to suit himself much better than another can do it for him, and many a one pays dearly for the experience which convinces him of his error.

In selecting a building site; in arranging the relative positions of the buildings to each other, and to the objects for which they are designed; in making such disposition of the different departments as will best facilitate the convenient and economical performance of the objects of use or pleasure to which they are devoted, taking advantage of natural features whenever they are available to save otherwise unavoidable outlay; having due regard to necessities of drainage, or other possible provision for health or comfort, to say nothing of possible future wants to which reference should be had, many problems are involved, the satisfactory solution of which demands the discipline of study and experience. Objects of utility or convenience may often be secured by availing one's self of natural advantages, which it would require a large outlay to attain by artificial means. Present or future wants may occur to the mind of one who has had the advantage of experience which might not suggest themselves to a novice, and a professional man might find means of providing for such wants which an inexperienced person would never think of. All these things are comprised in the essential duties of the landscape architect, independently of the artistic skill which enables him to preserve a unity of design throughout, and thus to give an expression of grace and beauty to the whole by the harmonious blending of its parts. The point I wish especially to impress upon the reader is that this primary work is what really confers character upon the place. Decorations of whatever kind may be subsequently added, and if tastefully and appropriately introduced, may tend to heighten the effect, or increase the attractive interest which pertains to the whole, but in no case can they render a place beautiful which is not intrinsically so, or atone for awkwardness, inconvenience or incongruity in the general arrangement, and moreover it is by no means impossible that elaborate ornamentation should destroy or seriously detract from the general expression otherwise conveyed, as for instance by conferring an air of ostentatious display upon an otherwise pleasant and attractive home, or detracting from the dignity of an imposing situation, by diverting the attention from the sublime or beautiful natural features, which are sufficient in themselves to excite admiration and occupy the attention.

In selecting the position for a house, which is to become a family homestead, on an estate comprising the usual variety of rural scenery, in the form of hills, valleys, wood, water, etc., either within or immediately adjacent to its own limits, it should be remembered that the immediate wants of its first occupants comprise but a single link in the chain of circumstances, which should be taken into consideration before making the final decision. The building about to be erected may outlast several generations of occupants, and it would prove a source of constant annoyance to discover, when too late, that an error had been made in its position, involving disagreeable consequences which might have been avoided, or failing to secure advantages which another situation would have afforded.

Such mistakes are very common, and a consideration of some of the questions involved will show that the probability of their occurrence is very great.

If any considerable elevation, commanding an extended prospect, is included in the area, the first impulse of an inexperienced person will be to select the summit as the most desirable site for the residence. The importance of securing such a view from the windows, as conducive to the happiness of the daily life of the occupants is apt to be over-rated in the enthusiasm excited by its first contemplation. Most people become indifferent to it, when its novelty is destroyed by daily habit, whereas the annoyances attending the access to an elevated position, which at first seemed a cheap price for the treasure to be secured, are never diminished by repetition. The necessity of climbing the hill at every return to the house, in all conditions of weather, through rain and sleet, and icy winds and broiling sun; whatever the condition of roads, mud or dust, ice or slush; under all circumstances of health and temper; suffering with a headache which makes life a burden; harassed with petty vexations, or hurried by unexpected necessities which no man escapes, renders it after a time so serious an evil that only the utter hopelessness of relief constrains the sufferers to submit in silence.

Better by far to select a less commanding position for the house, reserving the summit as an objective point for an evening stroll, when weather and disposition are favorable, under which circumstances the extended view will never fail to be appreciated and enjoyed. As a matter of taste also in securing the most agreeable aspect of the place from points of approach, the summit of a hill should be avoided as a building site, since a house thus situated has always a bleak, exposed look, especially if seen in whole or partial relief against the sky, whereas if the land rises in the rear of the house, the summit crowned with wood, and in front assumes the form of a gently sloping lawn, with groups of trees tastefully arranged to prevent the appearance of bareness, the effect will be to give a home-like and attractive expression, which every person of good taste will recognize with pleasure.

It is moreover not unfrequently the case that more attractive though less expansive views can be obtained from the lower point, by arranging plantations of trees or shrubbery so as to conceal offensive objects, and direct the eye to graceful or picturesque bits of landscape which are varied as the position is changed, and thus rendered more interesting than when seen in the single prospect from the summit which embraces them all.

It is not improbable that other and more serious objections may be urged against the supposed site than have yet been stated. The importance of reserving abundant room in the rear of the house for domestic convenience and pleasure, secluded from public sight, can hardly be over-estimated as an element of daily comfort, and if in order to secure the fine view, the house is placed upon the apex of a hill,— the ground sloping to the road in front so as to be fully exposed to view, and falling off in the rear also, so rapidly as to leave no room for domestic offices, wood yard, laundry yard, play ground, garden, etc., shut out from public gaze and amply large for all the demands of the family — the continual sense of discomfort and inconvenience resulting from the want will far outbalance the advantages gained. The position of the stable, both as regards its own requirements and in reference to the house, is a matter of essential importance. It should be convenient of access, yet not so near as to be in any way offensive; not prominently conspicuous, though I do not consider it an objectionable feature if unobtrusive, and it is all important that it should be capable of approach by a farm lane, instead of being solely accessible by the carriage drive past the front door. Advantage may often be taken of a side hill to economize construction by means of a basement in which the cow stalls may be constructed, with a large sliding door opening on the barn yard at a lower level than the stable and carriage house, and thus out of sight from the house. Much of the essential interest and pleasure derivable from whatever attractions the place may possess, is dependent upon so placing the house that the windows of the rooms which will be most occupied may command the most desirable views, and to this end it is of vital importance that the architect and the landscape gardener should act in concert, otherwise the portions of the grounds which possess the best capacity of tasteful development may be overlooked by the kitchen windows, while the parlors may command only a cheerless outlook upon the road. Architects would no doubt be more ready to join in consultation with landscape gardeners, if the latter were as a class more conscious of the duties and responsibilities of their profession, and better able to fulfil them. The question of an easy and graceful entrance drive by which the house may be approached from the road, and easy access to the stable must of course be taken into consideration in determining their relative positions, and also the subdivision of the land into useful and ornamental departments, of garden, orchard, lawn, wood, etc. And, finally, the arrangement of the plantations of trees and shrubbery requires the exercise of a degree of skill and taste which are never attained without study and experience. It is generally at this stage that the proprietor becomes conscious of his own deficiency and seeks the aid of a landscape gardener.

Tree planting is the first positive step in the work of redemption from the cheerless condition to which the place has been reduced, and if the owner has attained a conception of the possibility of a more graceful arrangement than that of formal rows, and attempts the arrangement of groups and irregular belts, he speedily becomes aware that he is going beyond his depth, and is fain to call for aid. He cannot satisfy himself in regard to their positions, and is utterly at a loss when he tries to imagine what will be the effect when they have attained their full size. Of their relative size, form and colour of foliage he has probably no idea, and if he attempts to stake out the ground for the planting of a group, it is probable that he will set the stakes within five or six feet of each other, and label them with the names of such trees as he has bought of a travelling agent, who has assured him of their desirable characteristics. He soon becomes sensible of a perverse tendency of the stakes, in spite of every effort on his part, to assume a formal character in their relative positions, which is very inexplicable. His determination was to stick them in as irregularly as possible, and he finds on looking them over that he can see squares, and triangles, and straight rows and quincunx figures continually repeated. And perhaps in the midst of his work he happens to cast his eyes into an adjoining meadow upon an elm which has been growing in undisturbed beauty for a century, and the thought flashes across his mind that he has been for an hour labelling stakes and sticking them in the ground as guides for the planting of elms, maples, ash trees, pines, hemlocks, and cedars, and there before him is a single elm covering in the spread of its branches a larger space than he has devoted to the whole group. The truth flashes upon him that he is working at a trade at which he has never served an apprenticeship, and he speedily arrives at the conclusion that it will be safer and cheaper to seek the aid of one who has learned the business.

Let me not be understood to say that there are not frequent instances of the exercise of the highest degree of skill and taste as evinced in the results of the work of amateurs who have had no professional training. To one such I am indebted for some of the most valuable lessons I have ever learned, but it is worthy of note that such men are ever the readiest to seek the aid of competent professional authorities, while inexperienced men will proceed without hesitation and commit the grossest blunders with a blind confidence that nobody can instruct them. On the other hand it cannot be denied that many of the so-called landscape gardeners are men whose practical knowledge is not governed by an innate taste, and whose pedantry and arrogance is the result of their ignorance on all other subjects. A little experience with one of this class is apt to prove so offensive that a man possessed of ordinary sensibility becomes disgusted, and prefers falling back on his own common sense, and working out the problem for himself with such aid as he may incidentally secure.

It will, I trust, be evident that this primary work of

arrangement which I have been describing is what really
constitutes the "landscape architecture" of the place, to
which all subsequent decoration is subordinate, and the
skill and judgment of the artist are shown in the tasteful
adaptation of the natural features to the necessities of the
case, and the attainment of the most graceful development of whatever attractive features the place may
possess, without any sacrifice of the obvious demands of
convenience. If the reader will consider the endless
variety of combinations of natural features upon which
it is the artist's province to operate, and the equally
varied tastes and necessities of humanity which are to be
provided for, he may perhaps obtain a realizing sense of
the demands which are made upon his taste and
ingenuity.

But apart from all considerations of the immediate
wants of the proprietor is the necessity of reference to
future possibilities.

This question is one of special importance in the West
and particularly in the vicinity of growing towns, where
land is rapidly increasing in value. It often happens in
a very few years that such a demand for building sites
may arise as will make it desirable to divide the estate
and set off a portion for the purpose of selling it in lots.
Even if the original proprietor does not wish to do so, it
may become imperatively necessary for his children or
successors, and special reference should be had to such
possibility in making the primary arrangement, and the
buildings and different departments so disposed that those
portions which it would be most desirable to set off may

be separated from the rest by opening a new road or otherwise, without disturbing the unity of the original place, or affecting it disagreeably, except by reducing its area. The importance of this will be readily apparent, and the necessity of exercising judgment and ingenuity in view of it, hardly less so. On the other hand, and almost of equal importance, is the possibility of external changes which may affect the value of the place or the comfort of its occupants, as, the probability of new roads being opened in its vicinity, or of neighboring tracts being made use of for purposes which may affect it favorably or otherwise. It is obvious that such questions possess an importance in a new and rapidly growing country which does not pertain to them in an older region, and every design for the arrangement of any considerable area should have reference to them.

CHAPTER III.

LANDSCAPE ARCHITECTURE APPLIED TO THE ARRANGE-
MENT OF TOWNS.— DUTIES AND RESPONSIBILITIES
INCIDENT TO THE WORK.— RECTANGULAR ARRANGE-
MENT OBJECTIONABLE EVEN ON LEVEL SITES.—
ILLUSTRATED BY REFERENCE TO CHICAGO.

F I have succeeded in showing that even in the arrangement of a private estate comprising only a few acres, there is abundant room for the exercise of practical knowledge and skill in the application of the principles of landscape architecture, no argument will be needed to prove that very much more intricate and elaborate problems must present themselves when the area is enlarged, and the tastes, interests and future wants of great multitudes are to be provided for in the laying out of a town or city.

The existence of sanitary, economic and esthetic laws which should govern the arrangement of cities, is abundantly proved by the penalties which have so often been paid for their transgression. We cannot plead ignorance in excuse for their violation, and upon us more than any pre-existing nation devolves the duty of their further development and application.

The opening of the lines of railroad across the continent has developed so much that was unexpected in the

resources and capacities of the regions they have penetrated ; has dispelled so many erroneous ideas in regard
to their susceptibility of improvement for the purposes of
civilized habitation, and has so facilitated the means of
adapting them to such purposes, that it has become a
task of almost equal difficulty to obtain a realizing sense
of the opportunities which are dawning upon us, or of the
responsibilities they involve.

The vast regions yet lying undisturbed between the
Mississippi and the Pacific comprise such resources of
wealth and variety of sublime and picturesque features
of natural scenery as can be seen on no other portion of
the earth's surface, that is accessible to civilization. This
is the raw material which is placed in our hands to be
moulded into shape for the habitations of a nation, and
such as we create, it must essentially remain for all future
time. All coming generations are to inhabit the cities
and towns, and go to their daily labors in the streets, and
seek recreation in the parks and pleasure grounds, and
be laid to rest in the cemeteries, the foundations of which
we are laying or preparing to lay, and whose essential
features of arrangement are immutable from the time
they are first occupied.

It may not at first sight appear that the duties and
responsibilities devolving upon us are materially different
from those which have attached to the similar work in
which our fathers have been engaged throughout our
national existence. A little reflection, however, will show
that the march of modern improvement has so altered
the relative proportion of means to ends, that the appli-

cation of the creative powers we now possess to the development of a new country, can no more be governed by the record of the past than the destructive agencies of modern warfare can be directed by the military tactics of a past age.

Before the introduction of railroads the settlement of the West was by a gradual process of accretion, a vanguard of hardy pioneers keeping ever in advance, enduring hardships and privations which could only be borne by men unaccustomed to the ordinary comforts of civilization. The better classes who followed were necessarily governed to a greater or less extent in whatever further improvements they attempted, by the works of their predecessors, and nothing approaching to scientific or artistic designs of arrangement of extended areas, based upon wise forethought of future necessities, was attempted. The Government system of surveys of public lands formed the only basis of division, the only guide in laying out county roads, or the streets of proposed towns ; and if the towns grew into cities it was simply by the indefinite extension of the straight streets, running north, south, east or west, without regard to topographical features, or facilities of grading or drainage, and still less of any considerations of taste or convenience, which would have suggested a different arrangement. Every Western traveler is familiar with the monotonous character of the towns resulting from the endless repetition of the dreary uniformity of rectangles which they present; yet the custom is so universal and offers such advantages in simplifying and facilitating descriptions and transfers of real estate, that any attempt at the introduction of a different system encounters at once a strong feeling of popular prejudice.

A new era in the process of the redemption and settlement of the wild country has now commenced, and a vast extent of new territory is annually opening to its advancing waves. Wherever a railroad is opened, all the labor-saving machinery and all the comforts and luxuries of civilization are at once introduced, and the newest settlements are equipped from the outset with all the physical necessities of civilized life.

The Eastern man who made the journey to the Mississippi thirty years ago found himself, after ten days or a fortnight's weary travelling by canal boat, stage and steamer, among a people differing in dress, habits and idiom, from those he had left; and if he departed from the great routes of travel and penetrated the interior of any of the Western States, he was forced to submit to inconvenience and discomfort for want of what he had always been accustomed to consider the simplest necessities of life, but whose names and uses were alike unknown to the majority of the primitive backwoodsmen who comprised the rural population.

Now the passage to the Pacific may be made in less time than was then required to reach the Mississippi, and without the surrender of any of the luxuries which have come to be regarded as necessities of modern travel, and which in spite of the tendency to vulgar display in the upholstering of hotels and public conveyances, have done good service in cultivating and refining the manners and tastes of a large class, whose only knowledge of them is derived from such sources. The traveler may now look in vain for the distinctive evidences of a primitive condition of social life. He will scarcely find even a log house, and nothing in the dress or appearance of the inhabitants or the furnishing of their dwellings will strike him as essentially different from what he has been accustomed to in the older settlements. Towns no longer grow up imperceptibly and apparently by accident, but are created as it were in a day, the population and material being furnished to order and delivered by rail at any given point, where they fall into place and assume their respective duties with almost the precision of military organization.

A striking illustration of the rapid conversion of the wilderness to an advanced condition of cultivation was exhibited at the last meeting of the National Pomological Society. It seems but yesterday that the convention was held in New York, at which that society was first established, and many of those who took part on that occasion are still numbered among its active members. At that time Nebraska was only thought of as a part of the great American desert, which was supposed to be incapable of cultivation, and within whose limits it was hardly safe for civilized men to enter except in armed caravans or under military protection; yet at the last meeting of the Pomological Society the prize for the largest and finest collection of fruit was awarded to Nebraska!

The change has been so rapid and so great that it cannot be fully realized except by those who can recall the various stages of progress from its condition of savage dreariness to that of smiling culture.

But in the arrangement of towns no advance has been made from the original rectangular fashion, which even when the site is level, is on many accounts objectionable while with every departure from an even surface, the advantages become apparent of adapting the arrangement of the streets to its inequalities.

Every one who is familiar with the river towns of the West will recall innumerable instances of enormously expensive works in cutting down hillsides and building up embankments; of the almost total destruction of valuable building sites; in one place by their being left in an inaccessible position on the top of a precipice; in another by being exposed to all the drainage of a street which is far above them, while all the naturally beautiful or picturesque features of the place have been destroyed or rendered hideous in the effort to make them conform to a rectangular system, as if the human intellect were as powerless to adapt itself to changing circumstances as the instinct of insects, whose cells are constructed on an unvarying pattern.

All these evil results might be obviated by due forethought and the exercise of judgment and taste in adapting the arrangement to the site; and now that we have reached the point when vast regions may be controlled by companies or individuals, and the sites and plans of towns can be selected and pre-ordained, it is unworthy of the progress of the age in science and art that no advance should be made in a matter of such importance.

If a town is to be laid out on any given tract of land, the first question in the mind of a landscape architect should be : How can the area be divided so as to secure the best disposition of the different departments whose necessities can be forseen and provided for ?

How can the streets be best adapted to the natural shape of the ground, so as to economize cost of construction, and attain ease of grade and facility of drainage, by taking advantage of the opportunities offered by nature to save expense of cutting and filling, while preserving the most desirable building sites in the best positions relative to the roads ?

How can any naturally attractive features, such as a river, a lake or a mountain, near or distant, be made to minister to the beautiful or picturesque character of the place, by adapting the arrangement to the development of their most attractive aspects?

Every one can see in the mere statement of these questions, (which are but samples of many which will readily suggest themselves), that the answers must involve possibilities of vital moment in a sanitary, economic and esthetic sense, and although the answers may be only approximately and conjecturally correct, it by no means follows that there is no room for the exercise of judgment. To pretend that their conditions can be best filled by an invariable adherence to the rectangular system, is as absurd as would be the assertion that the convenience and economy and comfort of every family would be best secured by living in a square house, with square rooms, of a uniform size.   The rectangular system has this in its favor, that the first cost of laying out is less than that of a more elaborate achitectural arrangement, because any surveyor can run out the lines, and morever, there is no way in which so many lots can be got out of a given area. By a parity of reasoning, square houses would cost less than more elaborate buildings, because any carpenter can build them, and they will cut up into rooms more economically than an irregular building. Yet people do not hesitate to pay large prices for elaborate architectural designs for buildings, which are to last at most for a few generations, while they suffer a town, which is to last forever, to grow up without an effort at adaptation to present circumstances or future necessities, while it is obvious in many cases that present economy involves enormous and irremediable future outlay or loss. The instances in which irreparable and inestimable evils have resulted from the violation of such principles of landscape architecture, as are indicated by the above questions, may be found in almost every city in the country, and the almost superhuman efforts which some of them are making to obtain relief, afford sufficient evidence of the importance of timely exercise of care for their prevention.

It may not at first appear that any very serious objection can be urged against the rectangular system when the site is a perfectly level one, but the consideration of a case in point, whose exceptions may serve as illustrations of the truth of the general rule, will prove that it involves the sacrifice of advantages whose value can hardly be estimated.

Chicago is situated on a vast plain extending in every direction for many miles beyond the city limits.

Probably no city ever had such an opportunity as hers to secure every possible advantage which the situation admits, by the exercise of judicious forethought in the preparation of a design adapted to the necessities which were certain to arise. Other cities have grown up by gradual accretion in a long series of years, but Chicago has grown from a mere village to an immense city in the course of a single generation, and many of her active and energetic citizens of to-day have shot wild game where now are located some of her busiest thoroughfares. Her founders were always sanguine of her future destiny, and from an early day declared their conviction that she would become one of leading commercial cities of the country. They had the history and example of all the cities of all the world to teach them the necessities, and warn them of the dangers which must arise, and which could never be rectified if not foreseen and provided for in the original design. The site was a dead level, offering no natural features to affect the design, except the lake and the river, the former comprising the only object worthy of consideration for esthetic effect, while the latter furnished a secure harbor for lake craft, and must of course always be intimately connected with the business interests of the city.

No evidence of special reference to these features appears in the original plan, and the only important provision which indicates the faith of the founders in the future greatness of the city, is in the breadth of the streets, which is generally from sixty-six to eighty feet,— a most important provision certainly, and one which is so often neglected, that it reflects credit upon the judgment of those who exercised such forethought.

Within the present city limits are comprised about eight hundred miles of streets, and with the exception of ten or twelve whose course is diagonal to that of the general system, and only one of which comes within a mile of the central business portion of the city, all the streets run due north and south and east and west. The town having originally started on these lines, the great city has grown up by simple projections of the same, the diagonals being old country roads whose convenience was too well established to admit of their removal. Before going farther, it is worthy of remark that the arranging of the streets according to the cardinal points involves a sanitary objection of no mean import. No fact is better established than the necessity of sunlight to the highest degree of animal health, and no constitution can long endure, without ill effect, the habitual daily privation of its health giving power. City houses at best can rarely be so well provided for in this respect as those which stand alone, as is generally the case in the country, and it is all the more important that every facility should be afforded to secure as much as possible of its genial influence. But every house on the south side of a street running east and west must have its front rooms, which are generally its living rooms, entirely secluded from the sun during the Winter, and for most of the day during the Summer. This fact, coupled with that of the indoor

life of American, and particularly Western, women, is
enough to account for a very large share of the nervous
debility which so generally prevails.   If the rectangular
system must be adhered to in city arrangement, it would
be far better that the lines of streets should be northwest
and southeast, and the cross streets at right angles with
them, than as now disposed.

The present city limits embrace an area eight miles in
length by five in breadth, and with the exception of the
few diagonal streets above alluded to, the city is simply a
vast collection of square blocks of buildings, divided by
straight streets, whose weary lengths become fearfully
monotonous to one who is under frequent necessity of
traversing them.

Here and there at wide distances from each other
single squares have been reserved for public use, and in
one or two of these squares an elaborate effort at decoration has been made by means of what is commonly
understood to be landscape gardening.   Mountain ranges
are introduced which are overlooked from the chamber
windows of the surrounding houses; lakes of corresponding size are created apparently to afford an excuse for the
construction of rustic bridges, which are conspicuous at a
greater distance than either mountains or lakes.   A light-
house three feet high, on a rocky promontory the size of a
dining room table, serves to warn the ducks and geese of
hidden dangers of navigation, and this baby-house ornamentation is tolerated in a great city which aspires to an
artistic reputation; the crowds which throng these places
in pleasant weather give evidence alike of the popular

longing for relief from the din and turmoil of the streets, and of the facility with which they might be made available for purposes of instruction by a truly artistic use of objects of natural beauty and interest.

A little area in the south part of the city, known as Ellis Park, is a pleasing exception to the general rule, making no such display of absurdities, and being beautifully kept and richly decorated with flowers tastefully arranged in masses set in a velvet sward. Few people, except those in the immediate vicinity, are aware that the city is indebted for the possession of this little gem to the enthusiasm of an amateur, who furnishes and watches over the flowers and provides for the wants of the trees and grass, and finds his reward in the gratification of his ruling passion and the consciousness of the pleasure he confers on others.

The reservation of the area now occupied by Lincoln Park was the earliest and most judicious selection of land for the purpose of public recreation, and it will always possess a peculiar and superior value and interest from the facts of its vicinity and ease of access to the business portions of the city and its position on the shore of the lake, which is the only natural feature of the whole region around Chicago, which possesses any distinct characteristics of sublimity. These are in effect the same as those of the ocean, whether in the idea it conveys of grandeur by its vast extent, of terrific power when roused by storms, or of living, sparkling beauty in its ordinary condition, when its rippling surface is dotted with fleets of sails and steamers. The shores possess none of the picturesque features which are essential to give the full effect of sublimity to an ocean view. There are no jutting headlands, no deep bays, no islands, or "cold, grey stones;" nothing in fact but an even line of sandy shore. The unbounded expanse of water, with its ever changing hues and moods, comprises in itself all that conveys the impression of grandeur, in which it is in no wise inferior to the ocean except in a single characteristic, and that is one which would only be observed by a practised eye. The heavy ground swell which is often seen in the ocean when no wind is blowing, and which is the result of storms so distant that no other evidence of them can be discovered is never seen in the lake. While its storms last, its breakers are as grand and terrific as those of the ocean, but the waves subside with the winds, and we never see, as on the ocean, a surface unrippled by a breath of air, but heaving with a solemn series of advancing waves which break upon the shore with a roar like thunder.

The lake is the one single natural feature which Chicago can command which possesses intrinsic sublimity and unceasing interest. In arranging a park upon its borders, therefore, it should be the objective point of attractive interest, the development and exhibition of which it should be the study of the artist to secure under such variety of conditions as would tacitly acknowledge its supremacy. The shaping of the ground and the arrangement of the trees should have reference to this end, and the drives and walks should be so arranged as to open views of the lake from different points, giving continual variety by the different framing of hills or foliage through which it is seen, but making it always the essential object of the picture. Instead of this, the park is cut off from the lake by a low range of sandhills which must be crossed before it can be seen. No art whatever has been applied to give a picturesque effect by the use of such accessories as would excite emotions in keeping with the grandeur or the beauty of the scene. The visitor crosses the hill and the blank sheet of water lies before him in its full extent, and all at once. No previous glimpses of portions of it, seen through distant openings between the hills or under an archway of overhanging foliage, awakens curiosity and excites the imagination by the intricacy and variety thus afforded ; and indeed, so far as any pleasure is derivable from the view of the lake, the park offers no advantages over the wharves of the city. Yet with this magnificent sheet of water at hand to furnish the key note of whatever improvements might be attempted on its shores, the prominent decoration of the park is an elaborately artificial lake which seems to have been constructed for the purpose of exhibiting a further display of such childish toys as adorn the squares. More rustic bridges, a miniature castle, and a grotto of imitation stone adorned with colored glass, the effect of which when lighted up, as a Chicago paper gravely informed its readers, "is quite equal to that of the celebrated grotto in Wood's Museum!"

To return, however, to the subject of rectangular arrangement, from which I have wandered.

If one has occasion to cross any considerable portion of the city on a line diagonal to the uniform course of the streets; that is: if he wishes to go from the north-east to the southwest part, or from the northwest to the southeast, he must of necessity travel nearly one third farther than would be necessary if he could take a straight course. The relief afforded by the few diagonal streets which exist is but partial, because they are not system-atically arranged to meet the necessities of the case, but they serve nevertheless to prove how valuable such a system would be, for they are always thronged, and the demand for business sites along their lines is far beyond that upon any of the streets in their vicinity. Except in the occasional instances where these avenues afford relief, the traveler whose course lies diagonally to the cardinal points, must traverse two sides of the great square which lies between his starting point and his destination. He may relieve the monotony of the straight streets by taking a zigzag course, but he can in no wise abate one jot of the distance.

Think now of the aggregate of unnecessary miles which must be traveled in the daily traffic of a great city, (and a city which may be termed a vast workshop, to which it may almost be said there is "no admittance except on busi-ness,") the wear and tear of the teams, and the loss of time which might have been saved by a judicious system of diagonal avenues.

Chicago is now preparing to spend millions of dollars in constructing a series of parks which are necessarily very distant from the thickly peopled districts of the city, because land in those districts is too valuable to be secured in sufficient quantities for such a purpose. The nearest park of the new system is between four and five miles from the Court House, and all of them are on the open prairie, and as yet far beyond the limits of any semblance of city streets. They are situated respectively north, west and south of the city, and are to be connected with each other by a chain of grand avenues or boulevards, having roadways on each side of a central mall, lined with trees and adorned with fountains and other objects of attractive interest.

The arguments most relied upon by the advocates of parks have been that they serve as "lungs to the city," by furnishing a magazine of pure air to supply the densely peopled districts, while they provide also a place of resort and recreation for the inhabitants, where they may seek relief from the turmoil of the confined streets in which their lives are passed in daily toil and refresh themselves with the sight of trees and grass and flowers. But how do these conditions apply to the case we are considering?

The streets of Chicago are all sufficiently wide to afford ample ventilation. There are no densely peopled, narrow, winding streets, courts or lanes; and if there were, what relief would they get from parks five miles off?

Doubtless in time those parks will be enclosed within the city which will grow up around and extend far beyond them, but it will be no population of laboring poor that will dwell in their vicinity. The palaces of the rich will surround and overlook them, and it will be only on an occasional holiday that the toiling denizen of the

central business marts, can afford the time or the means
to go with his family to those distant gardens.   That this
assertion is not a mere theory, is proved by the following
extracts from the report of the Central Park Commis-
sioners for the year 1872, which has come to hand since
the above was written:

"That large part of the people of the city to whom,
from the closer quarters in which they are most of the
time confined, the Park would seem to promise the greatest advantage, cannot ordinarily leave their daily tasks, at
the earliest, till after four o'clock ; nor their homes, which
in the majority of cases are yet south of Twenty-fifth
street, before five.   A visit to the Park, then, involves
two trips by street cars, which with the walk to and from
them will occupy more than an hour.   The street cars
on all the lines approaching the Park are at five o'clock
overcrowded, and most members of a family entering one
below Twenty-fifth street will be unable to get a seat.
Under these circumstances, the pleasure of a short visit
to the Park, especially in the latter part of a hot
summer's day, does not often compensate for the fatigue
and discomfort it involves, and accordingly it appears
that as yet a majority of those who FREQUENT the Park
are people in comfortable circumstances, and largely of
families, the heads of which have either retired from
business or are able to leave their business early in the
day.   Except on Sunday, and Saturday afternoons and
general holidays, the number of residents of the city who
come to the Park in carriages is larger than of those who
come by street cars and on foot."

And again : "It is obvious from the great difference in the relative numbers of people who visit the Park respectively in carriages and on foot on ordinary days, and on Sundays and holidays, that to the great body of citizens it is yet too difficult of access to be of use except on special occasions ; a large majority of the visits of ordinary short daily recreation being made at present by the comparatively small number, who can afford to use pleasure carriages or saddle horses, or of those from whose houses a walk to it is easy and agreeable."

That Chicago should even now provide for future certain wants, evinces commendable wisdom and exceptional energy and enterprise, but if younger cities will learn wisdom by her experience, and exercise an earlier forethought, they may secure results which are unattainable for Chicago by having their parks and boulevards as integral portions of the city, instead of being merely ornamental appendages.

CHAPTER IV.

AVING pointed out some of the defects arising from the neglect to provide in season for future necessities, I propose now to consider some of the advantages which might have been secured by such forethought; in doing which, however, I propose only to make general suggestions which may be equally applicable elsewhere, and which I trust will serve to prove the truth of my assertion that even on a level site the principles of landscape architecture (according to the definition I have given) may be judiciously applied to the arrangement of towns.

Let us suppose the central and most important business portion of the city to be surrounded by a series of small parks, connected by broad avenues or boulevards, tastefully planted and adorned with fountains, flower beds and appropriate works of art. Let other portions of the city, appropriated to special branches of business or manufactures, be similarly surrounded and isolated, and from each of these areas, let a series of boulevards radiate on lines diagonal to the general course of the streets, and extend as far as might be desirable, till they merge in other similar avenues, or connect with extensive outlying parks or suburban additions.

The effect would be that the inhabitants of every part of the city would find in these small parks and boulevards attractive pleasure grounds immediately accessible to their homes, to which they could resort when the toils of the day were over; suburban residents would enjoy the pleasure of a drive through a series of pretty gardens on their daily route to and from their places of business, instead of being forced to take a zigzag course through a series of monotonous streets, or travel a weary distance out of town to find a place prepared expressly for a pleasure drive and the saving of time, distance and labor, which would be secured in the daily traffic of the city, would in the aggregate more than compensate for the value of the land thus occupied. The beauty and attractive interest of the city in the eyes of visitors and strangers would be incalculably increased by the refreshing variety and superb effect of coming at intervals upon these beautifully verdant areas, and the importance of attaining such a reputation is rarely appreciated as it deserves. The attractions of a city do not alone consist in its architectural magnificence, or its sources of amusement and culture, though these are important elements. But in order to the full enjoyment of its theatres, museums, libraries, lectures and social pleasures, it is essential that the means of access to them should be rendered not only easy, and free from danger or discomfort, but attractive and elegant, so that the recollection of the enjoyment shall not be marred by an association of physical discomfort in its attainment. The annual increase of over 100,000 strangers to the winter population of Paris, is due quite as much to the fact that physical comfort and all the appliances of elegance and luxury are as carefully provided in the means of attainment of the objects of attraction, as in the objects themselves. Supposing each one to expend only $500 during the winter's sojourn, a total of fifty millions is added to the city's income, a reflection which is worthy the consideration of those who think it a waste of money to spend it for anything but actual necessities. But beside these advantages, the most important of all, and one which at this time will need no argument beyond its mere statement, is the obvious fact that the surrounding of the principal business and manufacturing districts of the city with broad areas planted with trees, and dividing the outer portions into sections by means of such boulevards as have been suggested, would constitute the best possible safeguard against any wide-spread conflagration. In every design of town arrangement, reference should be had to the danger resulting from prevailing winds of peculiar force, and so far as possible the risk should be averted or guarded against by means of intersecting open areas arranged with reference thereto.

I am of course aware that this general and incomplete statement of a system is liable to criticism, and many serious and perhaps some insuperable obstacles to its detailed execution will present themselves to the practical mind. I shall not enter upon the discussion of these questions. I do not presume even to say that in any case it would be possible to carry out such a design as I have suggested in all its details. My object has been to point out defects in preëxisting systems which cannot be denied, and to suggest principles by which those evils may be averted. How far those principles are capable of practical application, remains to be seen. It is certain that we have such an opportunity as no nation ever before enjoyed of testing and developing both the theory and the practice of the art.

Before taking leave of Chicago it may not be amiss to call attention to a lesson, the truth of which has been confirmed by her recent experience.

The opportunity of reconstructing the plan of a considerable portion of the city, before rebuilding upon the burnt districts, naturally suggested itself as too favorable to be suffered to escape, but the effort at its accomplishment resulted as all similar efforts have done. Before the ruins of London had ceased smoking after the great fire of 1666, a plan for the reconstruction of the burnt district was prepared and laid before the King by Christopher Wren, which was so obvious an improvement upon the old system of narrow and crooked streets, that a very strong effort was made to secure its adoption, but it was found impossible to reconcile the multitude of complicated and conflicting interests which must necessarily be affected, and no essential change was secured. New York had a similar experience after the fire of 1835, and Chicago now adds her experience in proof of the fact

4

that except under a despotic government, any essential
alteration of the original plan of a city must be regarded
as hopeless.

Since the above was written, the destruction by fire of
the richest portion of Boston has raised the same question
of the possibility of re-arrangement in that city. The
following article from the Boston Commercial Bulletin
contains so much that is pertinent and interesting in connection with the subject that I insert it entire :

DIFFICULTIES OF REBUILDING A CITY.

WHAT THE BOSTON MERCHANTS SAY.

As we predicted would be the case, the efforts of our Street Com-
missioners to secure the desired improvement of those business thoroughfares included within the burnt district, preliminary to rebuilding
it, are met with strenuous opposition from a large majority of the
abuttors. To be sure, their objections are of a purely personal character, and do not pretend to be based on any grounds of public policy ; but, nevertheless, they are of a very serious nature, and have
raised the question as to how far those public exigences which demand
the widening and straightening of these thoroughfares will justify our
municipal government in running counter to the private interests
involved in the undertaking. This question will have to be carefully
considered, not only to secure the ends of justice, but also, to save the
city from incurring an enormous addition to its debt in the shape of
land damages.

That these projected improvements will greatly depreciate the
value, for mercantile purposes, of hundreds of costly estates situated
in the very heart of the city, where building sites command almost
fabulous prices, there can be no question. Many of these estates,
with every inch of land and store room appertaining to them utilized

and crammed to their utmost capacity were barely large enough to accommodate the growing business of their occupants before the fire. Looking to the probable wants of the commercial future they needed to be enlarged rather than curtailed. But if they must be cut down, and thus rendered unavailable for the purposes of business on a large scale, to which they were formerly devoted, in order that we may have immunity from great fires, as well as wide and commodious streets running through from State street to the South End railroad depots, then their owners and lessees must be fairly paid for the personal sacrifices demanded of them. They cannot be expected to offset these sacrifices on the score of betterments because there is no such thing as betterments in these cases.

A widened street can be of no possible benefit to an abuttor, if it does not leave him land enough to rebuild a store on such as will accommodate his business. Besides, it is the opinion of many of these abutters, that wider streets, although they may afford greater facilities for through travel and transportation, will not offer any special or additional attraction to their local trade. It is also a notable fact that in most cases where they are ready to admit the public necessity of such street improvements, they still insist that the widening can most easily and cheaply be affected on the side opposite to that on which their own premises are located. Such an opinion, of course, is natural ; but then it shows that our merchants and real estate owners in that quarter of the city are standing in a defensive attitude against what they regard as an impending slaughter of their interests, and hence it behooves our municipal authorities to move with great caution and forbearance in the matter.

But while we would have them exceedingly careful not to take a single foot of land needed for private business purposes that is not positively required by the public exigences of the present occasion, and, moreover, do not believe that it is necessary to make every street running down to or parallel to our water front sixty or seventy feet wide, yet we would counsel no niggardly or penny - wise policy in carrying out a system of local inprovements which is to stand for all future time. These should be undertaken on a liberal but not extravagant scale, sacrificing nothing to the spirit of prodigality, but keeping in view the two great fundamental ideas of utility and progress. We must not commit the error of providing only for present emergencies, but must try to realize the wants of Boston commerce as it will be a century hence. The new business edifices to be put up in the burned district will probably be the most costly as well as the most substantial ever erected in any city on this side of the Atlantic, and after they are built it will be too late to think of making changes in our street lines. Whatever is to be done in this connection must be done beforehand, as the sad opportunity afforded by this great conflagration is not likely to be repeated in that locality.

But, after all that can be done to economize space for commercial purposes, the hard fact must still remain, that the business formerly accommodated in this burnt district can never be wholly put back there. Even with narrow streets its territorial limits afforded but a scant pattern and no " elbow room " for the great branches of trade which had been concentrated there. But after these contemplated street improvements shall have been carried out, it will be as physically impossible for them to get back bodily into their old quarters, as it would be to crowd a bushel of corn into a peck measure. They must hereafter be content to scatter themselves, and locate further up town, or wherever there may be a chance to spread out with the conditions of a healthy and natural growth. The Fort Hill district must be built up and utilized ; the old North end must be rejuvenated, and its antique structures give place to buildings suited to the wants of modern commerce. Even the retail trade must surrender its time-honored haunts on Washington and Hanover streets to the pressure of the wholesale business, while our central resident population must retreat before the march of improvement and find better and more pleasant homes in the outlying wards on suburban towns.

Whatever may be thought of such an arrangement as I have suggested, for a perfectly level site, it is hardly conceivable that any sane man will attempt seriously to defend the rectangular system when applied to a tract comprising much inequality of surface. Wherever it has been applied it has proved enormously costly, inconvenient and destructive of natural beauty. And yet the selfish greed of real estate proprietors prevents a departure from the practice, and renders them callous to the sufferings they inflict upon the future inhabitants, provided only that they can secure the largest immediate returns from the sale of lots, with the least possible outlay in preparing them for market. Recent experience has demonstrated in repeated instances that a larger outlay for a more elaborate and tasteful design for suburban additions has proved sufficiently remunerative to warrant farther investment in preparatory plans and improvements, and with such precedents it is to be hoped that the spur of self-interest will prevent the perpetration of such barbarism as has heretofore prevailed.

Take the common case of a town on a river bank, whose site comprises a level area of bottom land of greater or less extent, backed by a range of steep wooded bluffs, which are intersected at irregular intervals by ravines, diverging at various angles from the course of the main valley. Every Western traveler can recall instances of towns so situated, and the hideous results of the effort to force nature into formal shape by laying out the streets without the slightest regard to topographical features. The exercise of artistic skill and judgment might often render the peculiar natural features of such a site, the source of its most striking and attractive characteristic. The level land next the river is obviously the most appropriate situation for the commercial and

manufacturing interests, and the high lands which overlook it, for the best residences. The steep hillsides, if
preserved in their natural condition, or developed into a
more artistic expression of their natural characteristics,
by appropriate planting and culture, would form a strik-
ingly beautiful feature in the general aspect of the town.
Advantage should be taken of ravines to secure an easy
ascent to the summit of the bluff, and a fine avenue
arranged along its brow, which would furnish building
sites for the best residences, overlooking the lower town,
and commanding the views up and down the river.
Footpaths could be arranged up and down the bluff,
winding sufficiently to secure easy grades and taking
advantage of any natural terrace or " coigne of vantage "
to increase the picturesque effect by the introduction of
appropriate decorations : as a fountain, a monument, or
perhaps a rustic arbor and a bit of rich lawn. Thus the
face of the bluff which is commonly rendered a hideous
looking precipice, scarred with gullies, and unavailable
for any useful purpose, would become a chief ornament
and striking feature in the general aspect of the town.

The picturesque and attractive character which may
be conferred upon a town by thus making an ornamental
use of areas which are useless for other purposes, is
almost inconceivable to one who has given no thought to
the subject, and this may be very greatly increased by
attention to various little details, which are never even
thought of by those to whom the work is commonly
entrusted. Suppose for instance, as is frequently the case
in the West, that the site of a town is intersected by one

or more ravines, beginning a mile or more from the shore
of the lake or river on which the town is situated. In
many instances these ravines assume an exceedingly
picturesque and attractive character, attaining a depth of
a hundred feet or more, sometimes comprising at the
bottom a charming bit of secluded lawn, while the almost
precipitous sides are clothed with a fine growth of forest
trees, and in the spring are brilliant with the blossoms of
the trillium, anemone, blood root, and other wild flowers,
which seem to love to cluster upon such positions as are
most difficult of access. The invariable custom in laying
out land comprising such features, is to place the roads
at such a distance from the ravine as to admit one tier
of lots, the houses on which, fronting on the street, will
have their back yards running to the bottom or across
the ravine, the object being simply that the proprietors
may get paid for the land comprised in the ravine, which
is unavailable for any useful purpose. The result is
that all effect of natural beauty is lost to the general
public, who never get sight of the ravine except from
some point where a road is carried across it, and then its
attractive expression is entirely destroyed by the fences
running across it to mark the boundaries of the different
lots, as well as by its being made the dirt hole in which
every family deposits its accumulating store of old bar-
rels, boxes and battered tinware. If, instead of this, the
roads were carried on each side just on the edges of the
bank, and buildings only allowed on the opposite side,
the ravine would form an ornamental feature between,
on which the houses on each side would front, and the

residents on each side would feel a mutual pride and pleasure in keeping it tidy, and adorning it with trees and shrubbery. It is easy to perceive that such a street would form a highly ornamental feature in a town, the picturesque effect of which would be greatly increased by the occasional introduction of a tasteful bridge as convenience might dictate.

These few hints as to the application of general principles will serve, I trust, to illustrate my meaning and to prove that the element of beauty in a town as in a private place, must be integral to itself,—the result of architectural arrangement, and the development thereby of whatever attractive features its site may possess or command, and that it is only by the exercise of timely forethought in the preparation of a design, that these results can be secured. Subsequent decoration by fine buildings and works of art will of course serve to increase and promote the general effect of magnificence, but such decoration can never render a place beautiful which is not intrinsically so, any more than costly jewelry and elaborate dressing can confer beauty upon an awkward, plain and ungainly person.

Of late years the attention of capitalists has been largely drawn to the subject of landscape architecture as a means of increasing the value of suburban property, by the tasteful arrangement of large areas to render them attractive as building sites. In some instances very large sums have been expended in making improvements before offering the lots for sale; the roads being constructed in the most thorough manner, and ample provision made for sewerage, water, gas, etc.; and the road-sides and public areas tastefully arranged and planted. In other cases only the principal roads were opened, the lots staked and numbered and sold by the plot. In one instance which has come to my knowledge, the proprietor has himself built the houses before offering the lots for sale. From the best evidence I have been able to obtain, the plan of making all the needful arrangements before-hand, though involving a large outlay, has proved on the whole the most satisfactory in its results. "Supply creates demand," and purchasers seeing what they want ready at hand, with the assurance that no further assess-ments are to be levied for improvements yet to be made, are ready and glad to pay liberally for its immediate possession. The advantage of building before selling is that it enables the proprietor to control the style, and prevent the introduction of edifices of an objectionable character.

The success of such an enterprise must in all cases be finally dependent upon the architectural skill dis-played in its arrangement. Men of sense will not be attracted or caught by a mere ornamental design, show-ing that the ground is cut up into irregular blocks by squirming roads, which not unfrequently are supposed to constitute the attractive characteristic of the landscape gardener's art. A curve for the sake of avoiding a straight line, where the latter is most desirable, and no obstacle exists to prevent it, is contrary to common sense, which good taste will never violate. The test of the architectural skill of a design can only be attained by a careful examination of its adaptation to the ground. If it is then found that the roads are so arranged as to fit the natural surface, securing the easiest grades and leaving the best building sites in the most desirable positions relative to them, and showing that the objects for which they will be principally wanted, whether for business or pleasure, have been observed in their arrangement so that they will obviously facilitate those objects, then the essential elements of skilful arrangement will have been secured, on which the comfort and convenience of the occupants must be daily dependant.

Unless these points have been observed, the introduction of ornamental areas, lakes, fountains, etc., will not compensate for lack of common sense in the disposition of those features which affect the daily comfort of the residents.

In arranging suburban additions to Western towns it is important to hold out to purchasers the inducement of an opportunity to secure a return of investment by future further subdivision, and to this end the lots should be of such size, and so shaped that such subdivision may be easily made, without injury to the portion which the purchaser would wish to reserve for his own occupation. In every growing town of the West is to be found a numerous class of men of moderate means who are seeking an opportunity to invest a small surplus in a home for themselves, but who cannot afford to purchase solely with that view, yet may be induced to make an extra effort if the prospect is held out that a future sale of a portion may aid them in meeting subsequent payments. A simple division into rectangular lots of proper size for a homestead does not meet this demand effectually: First, because they are not large enough for subdivision, and, secondly, because they have no reference to the shape of the ground, which is often such that no portion can be set off which is in itself attractive, without serious injury to the beauty or convenience of that which is left.

The men who are desirous of making such investments are usually of the most industrious and thrifty class, and consequently such as it is most desirable to secure as permanent occupants, as a means of giving such character of stability and respectability to the place as will prove the most powerful attraction to others.

Here it is that the advantage becomes apparent of making the arrangement of the roads and lots conform to the shape of the ground in such manner that every desirable building site becomes available, without injury or inconvenience to others, which in case of inequality of surface or the presence of attractive natural features it is impossible to do by a system of rectangles. It is obvious that for the accomplishment of the object in the most desirable manner, the tract to be subdivided should comprise an area of considerable extent, and in most cases this can only be secured by the mutual consent of several proprietors. My own experience in repeated instances has given me confidence that proprietors of adjoining estates will generally acquiesce in a plan of improvement which commends itself when fairly laid before them, as being mutually advantageous; but on the other hand, it must be confessed that hardly any communities are free from representatives of the class whose object seems to be to profit by the labor and enterprise of others, and who block the efforts of their neighbors by refusing to coöperate with them.

It would be easy to point out instances of towns or villages possessing all the requisite elements of attractive development, but in which the efforts of the enterprising and public spirited members of the community have been completely thwarted by the swinish obstinacy of a single individual of the class alluded to. But such men have existed from the time Æsop wrote the fable of the dog in the manger, and we can only trust that like other vermin whose presence is offensive, they may serve some useful purpose of which we — and probably they themselves — are ignorant.

The point of essential interest in the experience of those who have undertaken the construction of ornamental suburban additions, is the evidence they afford that tasteful and skillfully arranged improvements are readily appreciated, and if wisely managed are very sure to prove lucrative investments.

Inasmuch as they add materially to the attractions of a city, and enhance the value of real estate in its vicinity, the projectors of such improvements should be encouraged so far as possible by liberal treatment on the part of municipal authorities. Even if the motive be only a speculative one the result is nevertheless a public benefit and every such effort should be facilitated by such public aid as may be legitimately afforded.

CHAPTER V.

CITY PARKS — LESSONS OF THE CENTRAL PARK — DIFFI-
CULTY OF SELECTING A SITE FOR A PARK — METHOD
OF RELIEF — ADVANTAGES OF A PLAN — PROPER MAN-
AGEMENT OF STREET PLANTING.

 CHIEF difficulty in all attempts at the creation of
a park in the vicinity of any city, has been that of
agreeing upon its location. The history of the
Central Park comprises some incidental features of interest, which may not be apparent to the casual observers. In
the first place there was scarcely any room for dispute as
to locality. If New York was to have a park at all, it could
only be in that direction. Singularly enough, too, the Central Park serves to some extent to corroborate what I have
heretofore said, of the effect of making ornamental use of
land which is valueless for other purposes. The land it
occupies was a series of barren ledges, of such forbidding
aspect that no one was tempted to incur the expense of
improving even so small a portion as was required for a
suburban residence, and its only inhabitants were the
hordes of squatters, whose shanties, clustering under the
shelter of the rocks, served only to heighten the dreary
aspect of the place. The land in the vicinity possessed
only a nominal value, and the prospect of its settlement

seemed very remote. The work at its inception was denounced by many short-sighted economists as a measure of indefensible extravagance, and all the steretyped phrases of abuse, which pertain to political blackguardism were brought to bear upon those who favored its prosecution. Yet in the ten years succeeding the commencement of work upon the park, the increased valuation of taxable property in the wards immediately surrounding it was no less than fifty-four million dollars, affording a surplus, after paying the interest on all the city bonds issued for the purchase and construction of the park, of three million dollars, a sum sufficient, if used as a sinking fund, to pay the entire principal and interest of the cost of the park in less time than was required for its construction. The incidental value of such a work as a means of attracting and diffusing wealth in the city is, of course, inestimable, but no more conclusive evidence could be afforded than can be clearly proved and stated, of the practical value of broad and liberal schemes of improvement which add to .he elegance of a city and render it attractive to visitors, while they strengthen the local pride and affection of the inhabitants.

On the other hand, the Central Park fails to supply the demand of the old and densely peopled regions of the city, for an easily accessible place of resort for pedestrians, and such a place in the heart of the city, New York with all her wealth will never be able to secure, and yet such resorts for those who have not the means to provide themselves with the enjoyment of nature's gifts of refreshment are certainly as important, and involve moral duties as onerous, as the provision of the more extensive driving parks for the wealthier classes.

Boston, in this respect, in her Common and Public Garden, comprising seventy-five acres in the heart of the city, is better provided than any city in the country, but Boston has no grand outside park, though she has abundance of admirable sites which are available. The difficulty is the one already suggested, that no one site will suit all parties, and any one party can block the game of the others. The case is by no means a singular one, and the readiest means of relief would seem to be the adoption of a system of mutual improvements between the city and its outlying suburbs, in the prosecution of which, the suggestions I have made in regard to the improvement of otherwise valueless land might be wisely applied.*

Instead of looking for a tract possessing intrinsically beautiful or picturesque features, let the city avail itself of any tracts which are intrinsically valueless, and proceed to adorn and render them attractive. Such places may be found of greater or less extent within the limits, or in the vicinity of almost every city, which detract from or destroy the value of adjacent property by their unsightly or offensive appearance, as being marshy or

---

*Since the above was written, I have received from Boston an "Essay and plan for the improvement of the city of Boston," by my former partner, R. Morris Copeland. The general design is precisely in conformity with the principles I have advocated — a series of parks connected by broad avenues, dividing the city into sections, and providing for those classes who are least able to provide for themselves, the refreshment of pleasure gardens within easy access of their homes.

composed of barren ledges. The Central Park has been cited as an illustration of the effect of improving such a tract in increasing the value of surrounding property, and a still more striking instance is that of the Parc de Buttes Chaumont, constructed since 1864, in Paris, which occupies the site of old abandoned plaster quarries. Before the park was made, the ground was an arid wilderness of clay mounds and excavations left by the quarrymen. By skillful management this has been converted into an exceedingly picturesque tract, comprising a lake, in the center of which rises an isolated rock more than one hundred feet high. Precipices of corresponding height rise from its shores, and are connected with the island by a suspension bridge, and all parts rendered accessible by picturesque winding paths. These precipitous heights are merely the remains of the old quarries, and, of course, their crevices and level areas have been provided with soil, and planted with appropriate trees, shrubs and vines, while the more level portions are arranged with carriage drives — the whole comprising forty-five acres of ornamental ground, quite unique in its character.

The improvement of such areas, which are worthless for other purposes, at once confers value upon surrounding property by rendering it attractive for residence purposes. If the plan were adopted by municipalities of securing and improving such tracts wherever they were available in eligible situations, even if they comprised but a few acres, connecting them with each other and, if possible, with outlying suburbs, by means of fine ornamental avenues, while the suburban towns themselves adopted a corresponding system so far as means and opportunities enabled them to do so, the effect would be to furnish a widely extended system of magnificent drives, expanding occasionally into gem-like gardens of irregular size and shape, and conferring a park-like character upon the whole surrounding country, which would exert a wider and more beneficial influence in cultivating and refining the popular taste than is possible by means of isolated parks to be visited solely for purposes of recreation. Such a system would afford, in fact, a greater extent of driveway, and probably through a greater variety of scenery than any city would be able to secure in a single park ; it would be readily accessible from all parts of the city, as well as the suburbs with which it would directly connect, and the expense of purchase, construction and maintenance would be less than that of a single area of equal extent, while it would be more cheerfully borne because it benefits would be more widely and equally distributed, while the work of improvement and consequent cost might also be extended over a longer period of time instead of being condensed, and enormously increased, as it must be, if its immediate completion is demanded.

Herein, in fact, is one of the chief advantages of a previously prepared design of arrangement, whether it be for a town, a park, or a private estate, since by means of it the work can be arranged in order of its importance, the most essential portions performed as required from year to year, and with the knowledge from the outset that it is always progressing to the accomplishment of a determined end, the unity of design being preserved throughout. Thus if the general design for the arrangement of the fine avenues and parks is determined, the work of preparation may proceed in order of importance, the first being grading and drainage, because until that is done there can be no planting, which is the most essential object of esthetic improvement. When the planting is done, further outlay for improvement may be postponed, or expended from year to year. Architectural structures and ornamental works of art can be added at any time, and may continue to be contributed as long as they can be tastefully introduced, but the growth of trees is the work of time, which can only be partially, and by no means satisfactorily accomplished by the modern appliances for the removal of trees of large size. An immediate effect, it is true, may be thus secured at a very large cost, but the trees thus removed will never attain the grace and dignity of form and rich luxuriance of foliage which comprise the essential elements of their beauty and character.

No such thing as a system of street planting under municipal regulation has, to my knowledge, been adopted by any city in the country. Every proprietor of a lot claims, and is allowed, the right of planting what he pleases in front of his own premises, and the result, of course, is an utter deficiency of the symmetrical and imposing effect which might be secured by the practical application of an artistic design. No two proprietors act in concert in the selection of variety or size of trees. One man pays a high price to secure two or three large elms, brought from the woods, where they have run up tall and spindling, with a tuft of branches at the top, which are cut back to stumpy projecting prongs, to correspond to the necessary mutilated condition of the roots. Such trees may survive, and even send out a luxuriant growth of spray and foliage, but the natural characteristics of the tree are lost and can never be fully recovered, and the chances are that it will exhibit from the outset only a meagre and sickly appearance. His next neighbor, perhaps, goes to a nursery and gets half a dozen maples, horse chestnuts or ash trees, and plants them all on a space no larger than would be covered by a single one of either variety when fully grown. The next plants no trees outside his front area, but crowds that enclosure with evergreens, which, if they ever attain half their natural size, will be pressing into his windows on one side and interfering with the sidewalk on the other, while long spaces are left vacant on which no planting whatever is done. The value and importance of trees as a means of increasing the beauty and attractive character of a fine street, requires no stronger argument than the fact that even such a helter-skelter, unmeaning and slovenly style of planting as the above, if continued for sufficient distance to give an appearance of general verdure to the view up or down the street, excites an involuntary emotion of pleasure in the mind of the observer; but few people who have not seen it can realize how much this is increased if the work has been systematically done according to design, the varieties of trees being selected according to natural characteristics of form and foliage, and the individual trees being of uniform size and sym-

metrical form. But in order to the possibility of such a
system, it is necessary not only that the whole work of
street planting should be under the direction of a competent superintendent, acting by municipal authority, but also
that he should have at command a nursery of such extent
as to furnish abundant supplies of trees grown and pruned
expressly for the purpose, so that any desirable number
of the same size and general form, of any given variety,
can be furnished to order and a whole street planted at
once. The nursery, therefore, should also belong to the
city, and be under the direction of the city forester. The
cost to individuals would be trifling, just as the cost of
water is insignificant when furnished by the city, in comparison with what it would be if every man had to supply
himself, and if the increased elegance and beauty, which
may be thus secured, could be generally appreciated, the
measure would commend itself to all who had a reason-
able degree of local pride and affection.

" The greatest part of the beauty of Paris is due to her
gardens and her trees. She is, indeed, a city of palaces ;
but which is the most attractive, the view up that splendid
avenue and garden stretching from the heart of the city
to the Arc de Triomphe, or that of the finest architectural
features of Paris ? What would the new boulevards of
white stone be without the softening and refreshing aid of
those long lines of well cared-for trees that everywhere
rise around the buildings ? The makers of new Paris —
who deserve the thanks of all the filthy cities of the world
for setting such an example — answer these questions by
pulling down close and filthy quarters where the influen-

ces of sweet air and green trees were never felt and the sun could scarcely penetrate, and turning them into gems of bosky verdure and sweetness; by piercing them with long wide streets flanked with lines of green trees; and in a word, by relieving in every possible direction man's work in stone with the changeful and ever pleasing beauty of vegetable life. In Paris public gardening is not confined to parks in one end of the town, and absent from the places where it is most wanted. It follows the street builders with trees, turns the little squares into gardens unsurpassed for good taste and beauty, drops down graceful fountains here and there, and margins them with flowers; it presents to the eye of the poorest workman every charm of vegetation, it brings him pure air, and aims directly and effectively at the recreation and benefit of the people."

The above extract, from a most charming and instructive book, " The Parks, Promenades and Gardens of Paris," by W. Robinson, F. L. S., conveys in a few words the idea I am endeavoring to impress upon the reader, that the elements of beauty should be everywhere present, pervading all portions of the city as an essential ingredient, instead of being confined to a point which is set apart expressly for the purpose.

No man who has the least love of natural beauty can fail to admire a fine specimen of a tree, even before it has attained the majestic dignity which age alone can confer. If its form is symmetrical, its trunk well proportioned to the mass of branches and spray which it has to support, and its foliage luxuriant and vigorous, conveying the idea of exuberant health, it is always a beautiful object and never fails to excite an emotion of pleasure. A street lined on each side with such trees of a corresponding size, would possess an intrinsic beauty, which would add incalculably to whatever architectural elegance it might possess, and would go far to make up for any deficiencies in that respect. Variety might be secured by changing the character of the mass, but not by an indiscriminate mixture of different kinds of trees, which destroys all symmetrical effect, and in fact fritters away the sense of variety.

Let any one observe the character of individual trees such as are generally planted in our city streets, and mark also the general effect and try to contrast it in his mind with the possibility above suggested. He will very rarely find a tree possessing any real beauty of its own, and very many, and especially of those of large size which have been removed at great cost, are not only utterly deficient in grace and symmetry of form, but present such a meagre and sickly display of foliage as can excite no feeling of pleasure in the mind. With such deficiency of attractive interest in the individual specimens, and with an utter lack of system in planting, it is by no means surprising that no effect is produced which is worthy of attention as conferring any distinct expression.

The large sums which are annually expended in all our cities in tree-planting, are in fact wasted so far as the results attained will compare with what might be secured by a more judicious system, and it is one of the inconsistencies resulting from general ignorance of the subject, that a matter of such vital importance to the beauty and attractive interest of the city should be left uncared for. Every city should own or control its own nurseries, in which the best varieties of trees for street-planting should be grown at such distance apart as would insure a healthy development, and pruned and trained in symmetrical form till they attained a proper size for planting in their final positions. The whole work of planting, including the selection and arrangement of varieties, should be under the direction of a competent superintendent, who should also be responsible for their subsequent care and culture. The care of all public areas, and their decoration with trees, shrubbery and flowers, should be entrusted to the same officer. If competent to the duties of the position and faithful in their performance, he might confer upon the city a character of refined elegance which is unattainable without such aid by any degree of architectural display.

While on the subject of street decoration it will be in place to allude to the very great addition to their attractive appearance, which might be secured, on such streets and avenues as are occupied by residences standing a few feet back from the sidewalk, by the entire abolition of front fences, or area railings. These fences and gates are often very costly and always very ugly, and as it is very rare that two of the same pattern are in juxtaposition, the effect of the whole is only that of an infinite variety of ugliness. If all these fences were removed, and the front area left open to the street, bounded only by a curbing rising a few inches above the sidewalk, the sod inside lying flush with its surface, the view of the houses would be relieved of a feature which never fails to mar the effect of whatever architectural beauty they may possess, the areas themselves would form beautiful additions to the attractions of the street by giving a rich finish to its sides, and the apparent width of the streets would be increased by the depth of the areas on each side. In the progress of taste and civilization, men are gradually coming to perceive that fences, under any circumstances, are objectionable, and are only endurable as matters of necessity, when they should be as simple and inconspicuous as possible. They have been banished from cemetery lots, which they have so long been suffered to disfigure, and often at enormous cost to the proprietors. They have disappeared from all the public squares and small parks in New York City, and the additional beauty conferred by their removal is almost incredible. The next step will be the removal of area railings, and I am confident the day is near at hand when we shall wonder that we could ever have expended so much money to injure so greatly the appearance of our streets.

CHAPTER VI.

IMPORTANCE OF THE WORK WE HAVE TO DO IN PRE-
PARING THE NEW COUNTRY FOR CIVILIZED HABITA-
TION — LANDSCAPE ARCHITECTURE THE ART WHICH
LIES AT ITS FOUNDATION.

HE world is always wondering at the exhibition
of the last evidence of human skill, enterprise and
power. The public works, the palaces, hotels,
steamboats and ships, which in their day are described as
magnificent triumphs of ingenuity and energetic enterprise,
but which in the opinion of croakers must prove ruinous
to their projectors, are found in a very few years to be
inadequate to the public necessity, and are so far eclipsed
by the new creations which that necessity inspires, that
they sink into comparative insignificance.

And the same is true of the growth of new cities. To
some of us who are not yet decrepid, it seems but yesterday
that travellers who had penetrated by weary stage journey
into the wilds of Western New York, came back with
enthusiastic accounts of the wonderful city of Rochester,
which had sprung into being in a day and attained civic
rank while the stumps were still standing in the streets.
Then came Buffalo, and Cincinnati and Chicago, each
outstripping the other, and each confident that it was the

Ultima Thule. But each has found itself the stepping stone to regions of greater and more varied resources, demanding more expansive systems of development. Chicago in a single generation has risen from an obscure village to be the greatest lumber market, the greatest grain market, and the greatest provision market, not in the United States alone, but in the world. What is the explanation? Simply that the wealth of production already developed in the regions of which she is the depot of supply and distribution, is greater than is elsewhere concentrated at any one point. But those regions are but thinly settled in comparison to their capacity; their productive powers are not yet half developed, and their whole area is insignificant in comparison with what still lies beyond unappropriated and valueless till its latent powers are touched by the magic wand of labor.

The burning of Chicago is simply the destruction of the depot of the railroads which concentrate there, and the means at command for her reconstruction are the combined wealth of all the regions traversed by those roads The energy and enterprise with which she is again springing up from her ashes, is based upon such knowledge of the value of those resources as inspires the fullest confidence of lucrative returns. It astonishes the world because there is no precedent by which a realizing sense of the measure of those resources can be obtained. And if this is true of the regions now tributary to Chicago, which have grown up with her and of which she is the just exponent, how much more difficult is it to obtain an idea of all that lies beyond.

It is only by comparison with some standard whose proportions have assumed a definite form in the mind, that any approach to a conception of the vast area which still remains unoccupied between the Mississippi and the Pacific can be obtained. The statement of its contents in acres or square miles conveys no impression whatever. Even an inspection of such portions of it as are already accessible, serves to aid the mind to grasp the idea of its extent only when the comparative insignificance of what has been seen is proved by reference to maps showing its relative proportion to the whole.

The traveler approaching from the East is impressed with the sense of solemn grandeur inspired by the vast extent and dreary monotony of the great plains. He flies by day and night over a road so level and straight as to admit the full speed of steam power, seeing no change in the boundless expanse on every side, save when he crosses the sandy beds into which great rivers have sunk exhausted in the effort to span the weary distance. He recalls the fact that he is crossing the plains at the narrowest point, and tries in vain to conceive of their transverse extent from their unknown limits in the frozen North to their Southern boundaries in Mexico.

All this region which till a comparatively recent date has been supposed to be a desert and incapable of cultivation, requires only forest culture, to restore the humidity of climate, which is all that is needed to develop its capacity of production. The possibility of forest culture has been abundantly proved at various points, and especially by the experimental nurseries established by **Mr. R. S. Elliott** on the line of the Kansas Pacific Railroad. The railroad companies are adopting measures for the prosecution of the work of tree planting on a scale commensurate with its acknowledged importance. Meantime individuals and colonies are everywhere penetrating the borders of the vast region, and like the silent and insensible process of cellular growth, the germ is expanding which we know must result in their final complete occupation.

The vague sense of solemnity resulting from the simple impression of vast, inconceivable extent, in crossing these regions is almost appalling. But the continued, solemn monotone seems but the appropriate and fitting prelude to the glorious revelation at its close, when all at once, as if by magic, the whole Western sky is filled with the grand outline of the Rocky Mountain chain, the majestic forms of their great spurs thrown out upon the plains like outposts guarding the flanks of the deep gorges which give access to the mystic land beyond, while in the far distance the sky is fretted with the endless variety of mountain forms and snow-clad ranges, which impress upon the mind the conviction that the vast plains which have just been traversed are only justly proportionate as the pedestal of so grand a monument.

The combined area of all the States east of the Mississippi is less than that of the regions which still lie unappropriated to the use of civilized man between that river and the Pacific Ocean. Portions of it have filled up rapidly since the opening of the Pacific railroads, and thriving towns and cities have sprung up where but yesterday was the home of the Indian or the trapper. The traveler is astonished at finding such a population, supplied with all the refinements and luxuries of civilization, in the regions whose names have always been synonymous in his mind with scenes of savage loneliness, and traveling only on the easily accessible routes which have been thus occupied, he is apt to imagine that the most important part of the work is already done, but the idea thus attained of the extent already settled is the best possible standard to enable the mind to grasp the conception of that which remains, when by reference to the map the comparative insignificance of the former is discovered.

Year by year the advancing tide of civilization is forcing its way by new routes into this region of mystery and beauty. Year by year new lands are appropriated and the work of preparation for human habitation commenced, and year by year the sites are selected on which new towns and cities are to grow up and form the central points of supply and distribution of the regions around, which will teem with a dense population.

We know that all this region of untold wealth which is our heritage, will at no distant day be intersected by railroads, its treasures of mineral and vegetable wealth attracting to it an enterprising and industrious class of inhabitants, while its wonderful developments of sublime and beautiful natural features will render it a central field of attractive interest for the pleasure seekers of the whole world.

We know that the health, and the daily comfort and convenience of countless millions who are to inhabit the towns and cities which are to grow up through all this region, may be affected for ages after we are forgotten, by the care or the carelessness with which we perform our duty in designing their primary arrangement.

The site selected may comprise within its area natural features for whose possession, for esthetic use, old cities would gladly expend millions, were it possible for millions to purchase them; it may command views of mountains, lakes or rivers, which lovers of the picturesque would traverse half the globe to see. The value of such possessions to the future town or city which is to arise on that spot is no more within the compass of estimate than that of the love which has created the beautiful in nature, and bestowed upon man the power to enjoy it. Yet this priceless opportunity may be lost forever for want of an appreciative eye to detect its value. The gem may be thrown aside as worthless, because no one is at hand to detect its lustre and arrange its setting.

The duty of laying out the towns is entrusted to a surveyor, and is comprised in measuring and staking out a certain number of streets at stated distances apart, running north and south, and east and west, and then preparing a " plat " of the same, on which the blocks are divided into lots which are numbered, and sold to the highest bidder. No regard is paid to the topography of the ground; no reference is had to future interests or necessities of business or pleasure ; no effort is made to secure the preservation of natural features which in time might be invaluable as a means of giving to the place a distinct and unique character. Even the certainty that where there is life there must also be death, is never recognized by such previous provision of a properly arranged place of burial as would seem simply consistent with a decent sense of propriety. In short, there is not the slightest recognition of the existence of such an art as landscape architecture. On the line of every railroad which penetrates the new regions of the West this mechanical process of manufacturing and selling towns is going on, and year after year they are becoming forever crystalized in their angular forms by the advent of purchasers to whom the deeds are passed.

Of course "nobody is to blame." The railroad companies must regard the interests of the stockholders, which require a rapid sale and settlement of the lands, to secure which they must be put at the lowest possible price, and that can only be done by the wholesale process of manufacture which has been described. The first purchasers are rarely of a class to appreciate any esthetic advantages which might be secured, and still less would they be willing to pay for possible benefits to their successors, and if purchasers would decline to pay the increased cost of having their towns made to order and fitted tastefully to the situation, the proprietors must provide the machine-made article; and thus, as in other branches of manufacture, the best quality is driven from the market.

Nevertheless the fact remains, that unless a change of the present system is brought about, the next century will

behold a continued series of towns dotting the whole
region from the Mississippi to the Pacific constructed on
the one invariable rectangular pattern.   Throughout all
varieties of natural scenery; the boundless plain; the
picturesque bluffs, commanding gorgeous views of lake
or river scenery; the sublime ranges of mountains, glit-
tering with snow-clad peaks, smiling with green and
fertile valleys, frowning with deep cañons; cities, towns
and villages are to be everywhere the same except in
size.   It is idle to say that "these matters will regulate
themselves."   They have not as yet given such evidence
of a desire for something better, as is indicated by a consciousness of present error; as witness San Francisco,
laid out in squares without the slightest reference to the
inequalities of her site; witness Denver, laid out in
squares on a gracefully rounded hill, commanding such a
mountain view as is worth crossing the Atlantic to see,
but of which no entire view can be obtained from any
one point within the city; whereas if a fine boulevard
had been arranged circling the hill, it would for all future
time have furnished so magnificent a drive, and such a
site for residences, commanding the whole mountain
chain from Long's to Pike's Peak as would have given a
distinct character to the city, and would have brought
more wealth to it — and what is better, more men and
women of refined taste and culture, — than all the
temples of mammon which are established forever on
the site; and witness the multitudes of towns laid out in
squares on the bottoms and bluffs of the Mississippi and
Missouri rivers, the founders of which have bequeathed

to all future generations of inhabitants a legacy of taxation, to preserve the hideousness of the original outrage on common sense and natural beauty, when a proper adaptation of the streets and subdivisions to the natural shape of the ground, would have made of the now unsightly bluffs the most striking and attractive feature in the general aspect of the town.

Only a few years since the beautiful island which divides the Falls of St. Anthony could have been secured by the thriving city of Minneapolis, which overlooks it, for a trifling sum, and would have made a park of a perfectly unique and rarely attractive character, but the opportunity was lost and is now never alluded to but with regret.

Day after day is bringing similar opportunities and silently offering them for our acceptance. No flaming advertisements set forth their merits ; no solicitations are made to us to secure them. We have but to reach out our hands, and they are given to us " without money and without price." But the solemn procession never stops or falters in its silent course, and if we miss the auspicious hour, the chance is gone forever. We may cast our longing eyes upon its retreating form, and curse our own blindness and stupidity, but it is as utterly beyond recall as the day in whose arms it was borne.

It may be said that it cannot be foretold at the outset what is to be the size of a town, or what will constitute its principal branches of business or manufacture, without which knowledge it is impossible to adapt its arrangement to its possible necessities. I have elsewhere conceded

6

this, in saying that some of the problems involved can only be approximately or conjecturally answered. The art of town arrangement is one which has as yet had comparatively little opportunity of being reduced to fixed laws, and the responsibility devolves upon us in connection with the work we have in hand, of developing those laws and reducing them so far as may be to a system. Ought we not to deem it a privilege that the opportunity is afforded us of establishing the principles of an art, which in the application we are enabled by modern science to make of its practice, should outrank in grandeur, and capacity of sublime and beautiful combinations, the utmost efforts of those which have heretofore monopolized the title of fine arts? For surely this is not claiming too much for an art whose possible compass may include the grandest features of natural scenery, and the noblest specimens of architectural skill, as mere ingredients, the harmonious blending of which for the development of their best effects, is the province of the landscape architect.

Certainly no people ever before possessed such facilities as are placed in our hands for carrying through to a successful result a pre-arranged plan of town construction, and no people ever before had such control of all the requisite material for the purpose. We have our choice of sites in a virgin region, comprising every variety of soil, climate, and topographical character.

Wherever a railroad is opened all the labor-saving machinery, and all the comforts, necessities, and luxuries of civilized life may be at once introduced. Mills, shops, factories, machinery and operatives, with houses for them to live in, may be delivered to order at any given point, and indeed are ready and waiting to present themselves at any point which offers sufficient attractions; and the question is certainly worthy of consideration, whether a judiciously prepared design, adapted to the natural features of the situation, and, so far as a judgment might be formed, to the probable necessities of the inhabitants, might not in itself constitute a very powerful attraction.

It is surely not impossible, on an extended line of railroad, to fix upon localities possessing natural advantages of such a character, and bearing such relation to the surrounding country, as must render their future attainment of civic importance almost a matter of certainty, and it would certainly tend to promote the object, if provision were made for future necessities by the preparation of a design of arrangement which should secure the most economical and convenient attainment of the objects which are of primary importance, and at the same time the best esthetic effect of which the natural features were susceptible. It certainly would operate as a strong inducement to attract immigrants if such a plan were published, and they could see for themselves that their future wants and comfort had been provided for, and while the enterprising and industrious classes who would be the first inhabitants, would develop the resources which would give vital energy to the population, the provision which had been reasonably made for taking such advantage of natural features as would give to the place a distinct character of refined elegance, by exhibiting an appreciation of them which would never be attained by a vulgar mind, would not fail to attract as residents or visitors the class of people whose culture and intelligence can alone confer upon a community the sterling stamp which gives assured value to wealth.

As a means of giving a generally attractive character to the country at large, the importance of securing a tasteful arrangement of the smaller towns and rural villages, is perhaps of even more importance than that of the large cities.

Sir Uvedale Price, in his Essay on the Picturesque, remarks :

"An obvious and easy method of arranging a village is to place the houses on two parallel lines, to make them of the same size and shape, and at equal distances from each other. Such a methodical arrangement saves all further thought and invention ; but it is hardly necessary to say that nothing can be more formal or insipid. Other regular plans of a better kind have been proposed; but it seems to me that symmetry, which in cities, and generally in all the higher styles of architecture produces such grand effects, is less suited to humbler scenes and buildings.

" The characteristic beauties of a village, as distinct from a city, are intricacy, variety and play of outline ; and whatever is done should be with a view to promote those objects. The houses, therefore, should be disposed with that view, and should differ as much in their disposition from those of a regularly built city, as the trees which are meant to have the character of natural groups should from those of an avenue. Wherever symmetry and exact uniformity are introduced, those objects which produce a marked intricacy and variety must in general be sacrificed. In an avenue, for instance, sudden inequalities of ground, with wild groups of trees and bushes, which are the ornaments of forest scenery, would not accord with the prevailing character. In the same manner where a regular street or a square is to be built, all inequalities of ground, all old buildings, however picturesque, will injure that symmetry of the whole, which must not, except on extraordinary occasions, be sacrificed to particular detail. Now, in a village all details, whether of inequality of ground, of trees and bushes, or of old buildings, are not only in character, but serve as indications where and in what manner new buildings may be placed so as at once to promote both variety and connection.

" There is no scene where neatness and picturesqueness, simplicity and intricacy, can be so happily blended as in a village."

These suggestions are applicable to multitudes of cases where new villages are to be laid out on sites comprising inequalities of surface, or natural features of an attractive character which might be made to contribute incalculably to the beauty of the town by conferring upon it the expression of rural quiet and natural ease, which constitute the charm of such a place, in distinction from the necessary formality of the city.

But what would Sir Uvedale, or any man of cultivated taste, think of the " formality and insipidity " of a western village, in which so far as possible every inequality of surface is made smooth, every street made straight, the houses placed on a line, and the natural growth of trees eradicated in order to replant in formal rows ? And if in travelling through the country he found everywhere a repetition of the same thing, every village a miniature city, differing from its neighbors only in size, or in greater or less display of pretentious public or private buildings, might he not justly feel the utter deficiency of an appreciative sense of the truly beautiful in nature, and be painfully impressed with the fact that a most important element of popular education was entirely ignored ?

That such is the impression made upon every man of cultivated taste is an easily ascertained fact. Of course the rule is not without exceptions, and moreover there are very few communities in which more or less individuals may not be found, who by precept and example are exerting a constant and powerful influence in educating the popular taste to a love of the really beautiful instead of mere tawdry or finical displays.

The apology always offered is the poverty of a new settlement and the demand for all the means at their disposal to meet the expenses of absolute neceessity.

But all the wind is taken out of that sail by the fact that true taste would be far less expensive than the present system, because it would leave undisturbed such natural features as could be preserved without actual inconvenience, and thus save much of what is commonly the most costly of the works of public improvement. The idea that an artistic arrangement is necessarily costly, comes from the almost universal misapprehension of the meaning of the term, which to most minds conveys only the idea of elaborate artificial decoration, when in reality the art consists in the development and tasteful adaptation of the natural features of the place to the objects to which they are to be devoted. The first cost of designing such arrangement is more than that of the rectangular system ; but the cost of the latter in its execution, and the incidental expenses attendant on and resulting from it, is often tenfold what the former would have been. Is it not time that an effort be made to instill correct ideas of what constitutes beauty, both by precept and example ?

We boast of our system of public education ; but the lessons which are learned in school comprise only the rudiments of the education which goes to make up the popular character. In how many Western towns may be seen a huge building which the inhabitants point out with pride as the college or university, with some high sounding title attached, and which on examination is found to be only one wing of an edifice, the rest of which is still in the clouds, but which is expected to confer a literary odor upon the place, and generally to promote its prosperity. The original endowment has been exhausted in constructing this fraction of the building, which of course is only a deformity while standing by itself. No means are left for improving the grounds around it, which are generally bare and neglected. Does it never occur to principals, teachers or boards of education, that if not inculcating a lesson that is directly evil by the example of extravagant outlay for an ostentatious object which is not half accomplished, they are at least neglecting one of the most important and valuable means of educating the tastes of their pupils, by suffering them to become

familiar with slovenliness and disregard of all effort to
give an attractive expression to the place where the work
of education is conducted? No impression upon the
youthful mind exerts a more powerful and lasting influence than that which is made by daily familiar intercourse with scenes of simple natural beauty, and the
man whose boyhood was passed amid such scenes will
find that he recurs to them in after life with a keener
sense of their loveliness, as he contrasts them with the
magnificence and ostentatious display which mark a more
artificial condition of life.

Whatever may be thought, however, of pre-arranged
designs for proposed towns, the importance of an early
attention to suburban improvements, is one which cannot
be too strongly urged upon multitudes of already thriving
and rapidly growing cities throughout the West. The
opportunities which are often available of attaining
possession of tracts of land, by the improvement of
which the beauty and attractive interest of the city can
be incalculably increased, while at the same time a lucrative return is secured in the form of increased valuation
of taxable property should not be suffered to escape.

The increase of population and consequent increased
value of real estate in Western cities is a matter which
may be said to be almost as certain as the laws of
nature. Different ratios of growth of course exist, but it
would be hard to find a town of 10,000 inhabitants that
is likely to remain stationary and easy to designate many
which will not stop short of five or ten times that number. Every man who has lived a few years in the West

can tell of opportunities he has missed of making investments in land which would have proved very profitable if he had only had faith that the ratio of growth would be maintained, yet the infidelity is not overcome, and the chances continue to slip by unimproved.

And so with cities, not one of which but would now pay largely to secure opportunities for public improvements which might once have been had for a song, but whose purchase would then have seemed a wild scheme.

But purchase alone is not enough. If simply bought and held for a rise, it may prevent neighboring occupation, and thus depreciate in value. Improvements must be added of such character as will attract occupants by giving evidence that a broad and liberal spirit has been exerted in providing for their welfare and comfort.

Hardly any investment is safer for capitalists than the judicious purchase and tasteful improvement of attractive sites for suburban additions, and such investments are becoming common by individuals and companies in the vicinity of many thriving cities, whose governing powers should second the enterprise in corresponding spirit by extending connecting avenues, and thus as it were appropriating them as integral portions of a grand system of elegant embellishment.

I have endeavored to convey my idea of the scope of the art of landscape architecture, and I do not think my general premises will be disputed. It cannot be denied that one mode of adapting the arrangement of a city, a town or a private estate to the natural features of its situation, may be preferable to another, as a means of securing the utmost convenience, in the most economical as well as the most attractive and graceful manner. It cannot be denied that the infinitely varying circumstances of the topography of different situations, must involve a corresponding variety of arrangement in order to secure the best for each. It cannot be denied that the design of such arrangement demands the exercise of skill, judgment and taste, equal at least to that required for the architecture of buildings. It seems almost absurd that such a course of reasoning should be necessary in order to prove the existence of such an art as landscape architecture, but while we continue to ignore its existence and to go on blindly and without method, in the performance of works which obviously should be based directly upon its principles — and with such an opportunity as no nation ever before enjoyed of developing the theory and practice of the art — am I not right in asserting its claims and demanding, if only for the sake of our future reputation, that they should be recognized?

The statement and solution of the problems involved in the practical application of the art, on the scale suggested would be inappropriate to my present object. The scientific discussion of the subject, (if the man could be found who is competent to it) would require a volume of such compass as would be likely to repel the class of readers I have most desired to attract. I have purposely avoided such statements of details as may be found elsewhere, and have hoped only to call attention to the momentous duties devolving upon us, which so far as I am aware have never been more than vaguely alluded to, but for the performance of which we are to be held responsible for all coming time; and to prove the existence of laws which must be observed if we would avoid the errors or secure the advantages whose effects for evil or for good are alike incalculable,— alike within our control up to the moment of execution, and alike unchangeable thenceforth and forever.

Forest Planting

on the

Great Plains.

FOREST PLANTING ON THE GREAT PLAINS.

UBLIC attention has been so frequently called of late years to the subject of the wasteful destruction of our native forests, and the necessity of adopting energetic measures of relief by means of an extended system of forest planting, that it is unnecessary to attempt to set forth its importance in stronger language than has been repeatedly used in scientific essays, in agricultural addresses, and in congressional speeches.

I propose, therefore, to avail myself of the evidence of well known authorities, in proof of the necessity of action and of the penalties invoked in delay, referring those who wish for more detailed information to the publications from whose pages I shall quote, and then offering such suggestions as to measures of relief as seem to me to be worthy of consideration.

In the well known " Report on the Trees and Shrubs of Massachusetts," by George B. Emerson, published by order of the Legislature in 1846, the following passage occurs:

" The importance of the forests as furnishing materials for ship-building, house-building, and numerous other arts, is so obvious that

it must occur to every one ; and yet there is danger that in many
places, from false motives of immediate economy, no provision will
be made for the wants of future generations. It is not easy to estimate
the value of the wood used in house-building. The thousands of tons
of timber, boards, clapboards and shingles, used in such improvements,
are not put on record. As to ship-building, we have some data. The
returns from the various towns in the State, made in 1837, show that
the average annual value of ships built in the five preceding years was
$1,370,649. * * * The effect of the wasteful destruction of the for-
est trees is already visible. A very large proportion of the materials of
ship-building, house-building, and manufactures, are now brought from
the other States. Every year we are more dependant on Maine and
New York, and some of the Southern States, not only for ship-timber
and lumber for house-building, but for materials for tanning and
dyeing, carriage-building, basket-making, last-making, furniture,
agricultural implements, barrel-staves, and wooden-ware of all descriptions. Even these foreign resources are fast failing us. Within the
last quarter of a century the forests of Maine and New York, from
which we draw our largest supplies, have disappeared more rapidly
than those of Massachusetts ever did. In a quarter of a century more,
at this rate, the supply will be entirely cut off."

The warning embodied in these words was suffered to
pass unheeded. The quarter of a century has passed and
the prediction has been more than fulfilled. The rate of
demand on which it was based has increased to a degree
which would then have seemed incredible; and while we
have still to regret the want of any record by which an
estimate can be formed of the amount of timber annually
drawn from the forests, or of the probable duration of the
present sources of supply, yet a consideration of the single
item of the timber required for railroad construction,
(which at the time the above was written was not of sufficient importance to demand notice), and give a moment's

thought to what it must be in the not distant future, we cannot fail to be convinced that the work of providing for it has become a matter of national importance which it were worse than folly to postpone.

Few persons not concerned in railroad construction have any realizing sense of the enormous draft it involves upon the natural supplies of timber, and few even of those so engaged have considered, as it deserves, the problem of the future supply for the vast region which is now opened to us between the Missouri and the Rocky Mountains, a country rich in various natural resources, but utterly destitute of timber, the one thing needful for the development of its agricultural and mineral wealth.

Upwards of 50,000 miles of railroad are now in actual use in the United States.

That their multiplication must go on in a constantly increasing ratio is as certain as that the population of the country must continue to increase. Every mile of railroad requires 2,700 ties, which in the West are mostly of oak, cedar or chestnut, and are worth at least fifty cents each, or $1,350 per mile. They are generally made of comparatively young wood, that is of trees not more than eight or ten inches in diameter, requiring only to be hewn flat on the upper and under surface. The average number of ties cut from a tree of this size is probably not more than two; but allowing it to be three, which it cannot exceed, we find the number of trees required to furnish ties for the railroads already constructed to be 45,000,000.

7

Estimating the yield of a single acre at 200 trees, which is a large allowance for the average yield of native woods, it will be seen that the produce of 225,000 acres will be required to furnish ties for the existing roads, and as the duration of ties is not more than eight years, it follows that the above area must be stripped as often as that to furnish simply the first article required in its construction after the road is graded. It is true that a better economy is beginning to prevail in some parts of the West, where railroad companies have purchased large tracts of forest and established mills for sawing the timber, so as to avoid the wasteful necessity of using only young timber.

The fact of the adoption of such a measure of economy is in itself an evidence of the sense of future necessities which impelled it. A consideration of future wants will show that much more efficient measures are required than the mere economizing of present supplies, in order to meet the enormous demand, of which the item I have selected for illustration is really one of minor importance, but one whose amount can be more readily expressed than most others. A moment's reflection will show that it comprises but a small portion of what is required for railroad use, in comparison with the demand for bridges, buildings, fences and rolling stock. And when it is considered that all this enormous consumption is but a small fraction of the aggregate required for the infinite variety of uses to which it is applied, it does not seem surprising that the supply is already approaching an estimable period of duration. The following statement is condensed from a very interesting essay, published in the transactions of the Illinois Horticultural Society :

" Timber, both hard and soft, is rapidly disappearing from our forests. At the present rate of denudation it will be but comparatively a short time until its price will be beyond the limits of the general industries for which it is now used. European countries have been drawing for years upon American forests for a large part of their supplies. Over 800,000 acres of timber are annually cut in the three great States of Michigan, Wisconsin and Minnesota, while but 150,000 acres are annually planted in all the States. In 1869, 1,750,-000,000 feet of lumber were sent to the lake ports of Lake Michigan from the forests of Michigan and Wisconsin."

Col. J. W. Foster, in his very valuable and interesting work on the " Mississippi Valley," says :

" In the United States the destruction of the forest is going on at an accelerated pace. The lumber trees of Maine, in accesible positions, are nearly exhausted, and twenty years more will accomplish the same result with regard to the extensive pineries of Michigan and Wisconsin. The white pine is the most valuable lumber tree of America. The ease with which it is wrought ; its freedom as compared with most trees, from shrinking, swelling and warping ; and its durability when properly protected by paint, make it the principal tree employed in the construction of a vast majority of houses, and even fences and sidewalks. To one who realizes how rapidly the sources of supply are becoming exhausted, and the prodigality with which it is used, it cannot but be disheartening. It is a tree of slow growth, and the surface on which it grows, when disrobed, is unfit for profitable agriculture. The annual receipts of pine lumber at Chicago alone are in excess of 730,000,000 feet, 400,000,000 shingles, and 24,000,000 of lath. Possessing a material within easy reach and on the banks of a canal, known as the Athens limestone, unequalled for flagging and building, and having a river whose dredgings are capable of conversion into brick, it is a singular fact which strikes every stranger within her gates, that Chicago should exhibit such an extent of wooden tenements and plank sidewalks — structures of the most superficial character, which must soon give way to those more solid and enduring. The products of the lake pineries are distributed over half a continent. From them are built the farm houses of the pioneers on the solitary prairies,* and the bridges which span the waters of the Kansas and the Platte.

" The destruction of hard wood timber is going on at a pace equally as rapid. The railways require annually in construction and maintenance at least 10,000,000 of ties. Nothing strikes the emigrant from the Atlantic slope, on returning after years of absence, so forcibly as to see those hills which in his youth were forest crowned, now bare and desolate, and the streams in which he was accustomed to fish dwindled into mere trickling rills.† The Pacific railroads which traverse for long distances the valleys of the Kaw and Platte, have consumed in their construction nearly every stick of timber, and in four years will have consumed all the firewood. The beautiful black walnuts of the Kaw valley, fit for gunstocks and cabinet ware, have been remorselessly sacrificed to these base purposes."

I cannot better conclude the evidence on this branch of the subject than by introducing the following report of a committee on Forest Culture, which was read at the last meeting of the National Agricultural Association in St. Louis :

At the recent meeting of the National Agricultural Association in

---

*In journeying last summer on the plains between Lincoln, Neb., and Fort Kearney, I asked a new settler at whose house I stopped to dine, where he got the lumber for his house, not a tree being in sight. The answer was : " I ordered it from Chicago to Lincoln by rail, and hauled it out from there (thirty miles) with my team." H. W. S. C.

†In confirmation of this statement I may mention that on a recent visit to a town on the Nashua River in Massachusetts, I was recurring to the delight I used to experience when a boy, more than forty years ago, in witnessing the wild scenes of the annual freshets when the intervale land on each side of the river was converted into an angry flood, when I was astonished to learn that nothing of the kind had been known for twenty or thirty years past — doubtless the result of the stripping off of the forests, to which Mr. Foster so feelingly alludes.
H. W. S. C.

St. Louis, a report of which we find in the Missouri Democrat, the following striking paper was read, having been prepared by R. S. Elliott, Esq., the well known Industrial Agent of the Kansas Pacific Railroad Company:

REPORT.

The Committee on Forest Culture beg leave to report as follows:
The forests of the continent are rapidly passing away. Large districts in the Atlantic States are already stripped of their most valuable timber. In 'less than twenty-five years the accessible forests in the region of the great lakes, on the upper waters of the Mississippi, and in the British possessions adjacent, will be exhausted. The industrial progress of the Southern States is consuming trees both deciduous and evergreen at an accelerating rate. In the Rocky Mountain regions (where the hard woods are unknown) the pines, spruces and cedars are disappearing before the farmer, the miner, the architect and the railroad builder. On the Pacific coast, the immense home demand, ever increasing, together with the exportations to England, France, Australia, China, Japan, South America, Mexico and the Pacific Islands foretell the exhaustion of the California timber trees in twenty years; and those available in Oregon and regions northward within a comparatively brief period.

The demand for the product of the forest constantly increases. The supply constantly, and in a growing ratio, diminishes, and prices constantly augment. The causes now in operation, and daily gaining strength, can have but one effect, that of exhausting all the available sources of supply within the lives of persons now in existence.

This appalling prospect, the view of which becomes more vivid the more it is studied, should arouse the farmers, land-owners and legislators. It is vital to the future welfare of our people that the reproduction of the forests should at once begin, not on a small scale or in few localities, but in large measures and co-extensive with our settlements. A broad statesmanship, in our national and State Legislature, should at once take up the subject, and deal with it year by year until the great work shall be adequately begun.

The few and hesitating experiments in isolated localities, which have been made in the growing of forest trees, have no significance as far as the general supply of future wants is concerned. But they are of inestimable value in so far as they teach the ease and comparative rapidity with which forest trees, useful to the farm, to the workshop and to the railroad, may be produced ; and in so far as they show that the agricultural men of the country have already (in advance of the men in high political life), appreciated the necessities of the present and the future. They are also of value in demonstrating that, however remote the profit of forest culture may have been heretofore considered, it is yet true that the artificial plantation may in a very few years, by judicious planting at first, be made to yield current returns equal to the cost of planting and care.

Modifications and ameliorations of climate, due to the destruction or the extension of forests, have begun to enlist serious consideration. There can be no doubt of the beneficial influence of the forest areas equal in aggregate to one-fourth or one-third of the entire area of any extensive region. But however important climate effects may be in this connection — however desirable it may be that the crops and animal life of the farm should enjoy the benefits of forest influences and shelter, the need of extensive forest planting is important enough without taking into consideration its effect on atmospheric movements, temperature and rainfall. The store, the dwelling, the shop, the factory, the railroad, the wharf, the warehouse — all these demand action ; demand it in the name of domestic life, of farm economy, of commerce, of all the arts of our civilization. What we shall save in climate by preserving forest areas, or gain by their extension, is just so much to be enjoyed in addition to other compensations. The less violent sweep of the winds in Illinois, as compared with forty or fifty years ago, due to the obstruction caused by buildings, hedges, fences, orchards, artificial groves, and wind-breaks on her prairies, speak to the understanding of plain men more forcibly than any language we could use.

There may be those who regard forest planting as a work of mystery and grandeur, beyond the reach of common farmer. This is a mistaken view. Nearly all the most important deciduous trees may be grown from seed as readily as Indian corn. Of many species the seed may be sown broadcast and harrowed in, if the planter prefers to use the seed lavishly rather than give more care. The seeds of many trees may be planted either in the fall or spring, as may be most convenient. Some of the softer wooded trees grow from cuttings as readily as the grape ; and with most deciduous trees, the seeds or cuttings may, if desired, be at once planted where the trees are to stand. Nor need the most unlettered farmer deny himself the pleasure and profit of the conifers and evergreens. The plants, furnished at prices which are insignificant in comparison with their value, are abundant at reliable nurseries, and with the simple precaution of keeping the roots moist, and proper care in planting, are as sure to grow as any other tree or shrub.

No part of the earth is blessed with a greater variety of useful trees. both of the hard and soft wooded kinds, than the United States ; and these native trees can all be readily grown in artificial plantations. It is not alone the pines and spruces and cedars that make up our valuable timber. The harder wooded trees — the ash, the oak, the hickories, the maples, the walnuts and the chestnuts — of which we have heretofore been so lavish, have a value in the arts that no figures can estimate. They may be said to be essential to the continuance of our present civilization. New forests of these trees must be grown, or our grandchildren must depart from our modes of life. West of longitude 100 degrees from Greenwich, the material of a common wagon does not grow on the continent, and we are fast exhausting it east of that meridian. Ohio and Indiana, Kentucky and Missouri, have girdled and burnt hard wood trees that to-day would be worth hundreds of millions of dollars. If failing springs and protracted drouths and extremes of temperature suggest replanting, their people may safely rely on a future market, more certain than for any other product of the soil.

To carry out the views embodied in this report, your committee submit the following resolutions for adoption by this National Agricultural Congress.

JOHN A. WARDEN,
R. S. ELLIOTT, } *Committee.*
W. C. FLAGG

Resolved. 1. That we recommend farmers throughout the United States to plant with trees their hilly or other waste lands, and at least ten per cent. of their farms with trees, in such a manner as to provide shelter belts or clumps, and rapid growth and useful timber.

2. That we solicit the legislatures of the several States to pass laws providing bounties for planting useful trees, encouraging the planting of the highways, and for the provision of State nurseries of young timber trees ; and also the appointment of an Arbor Day for the annual planting of trees, as has already been done in the State of Nebraska.

3. That we ask our Congress of the United States to require, so far as practicable, that hereafter railroad companies and settlers receiving the benefit of the homestead and other acts donating lands, shall plant with timber trees one-tenth of the lands so donated.

Concerning the influence of forests on temperature, humidity, etc., I make the following extracts from Marsh's " Man and Nature ":

" Sir John F. W. Herschel enumerates among 'the influences unfavorable to rain,' 'absence of vegetation, especially of trees,' and says : ' This is no doubt one of the reasons of the extreme aridity of Spain. The hatred of a Spaniard toward a tree is proverbial. Many districts in France have been materially injured by denudation ; and on the other hand, rain has become more frequent in Egypt since the more vigorous cultivation of the palm tree.' "

Barth presents the following view of the subject :

" The ground in the forest, as well as the atmospheric stratum over it, continues humid after the woodless districts have lost their moist-ure ; and the air charged with the humidity drawn from them, is usually carried away by the winds before it has deposited itself in a condensed form on the earth. Trees constantly transpire through their leaves a great quantity of moisture, which they partly absorb again by the same organs, while the greater part of their supply is pumped up through their widely ramifying roots from considerable depths in the ground. Thus a constant evaporation is produced which keeps the forest atmosphere moist even in long droughts, when all other sources of humidity in the forest itself are dried up. The warm, moist currents of air which come from other regions are cooled as they approach the wood by its less heated atmosphere, and obliged to let fall the humidity with which they are charged. The woods contribute to the same effect by mechanically impeding the motion of fog and rain cloud, whose particles are thus accumulated and condensed to rain. The forest thus has greater power than the open ground to retain within its own limits already existing humidity, and to preserve it, and it attracts and collects that which the wind brings it from elsewhere, and forces it to deposit itself as rain or other precipitation. In consequence of these relations of the forest to humidity it follows that wooded districts have both more frequent and more abundant rain, and in general are more humid than woodless regions ; for what is true of the woods themselves in this respect, is true also of the open country in their neighborhood, which in consequence of the ready mobility of the air and its constant changes, receives a share of the characteristics of the forest atmosphere, coolness and moisture When the districts stripped of trees have long been deprived of rain and dew, and the grass and fruits of the field are ready to wither, the grounds which are surrounded by woods are green and flourishing. By night they are refreshed with dew, which is never wanting in the moist air of the forest, and in due season they are watered by a beneficent shower or a mist which rolls slowly over them."

Asbjornson, after adducing the familiar theoretical arguments on this point, adds :

" The rainless territories in Peru and North Africa establish this conclusion, and numerous other examples show that woods exert an influence in producing rain, and that rain fails where they are wanting — for many countries have, by the destruction of the forests, been deprived of rain, moisture, springs and watercourses, which are necessary for vegetable growth. In Palestine, and many other parts

of Asia and Northern Africa, which in ancient times were the
granaries of Europe, fertile and populous, similar consequences have
been experienced.   These lands are now deserts, and it is the destruction of the forests alone which has produced this desolation.   In
Southern France many districts have from the same cause become
barren wastes of stone, and the cultivation of the vine and olive has
suffered severely since the baring of the neighboring mountains.   On
the other hand, examples of the beneficial influence of planting and
restoring the woods are not wanting.   In Scotland, where many miles
square have been planted with trees, this effect has been manifest, and
similar observations have been made in several places in Southern
France."

Monestier Savignat arrives at this conclusion :

" Forests on the one hand diminish evaporation ; on the other they
act on the atmosphere as refrigerating causes.   The second scale of
the balance predominates over the other, for it is established that in
wooded countries it rains oftener, and that the quantity of rain being
equal, they are more humid."

Boussingault, whose observations on the drying up of
lakes and springs, from the destruction of the woods in
tropical America, have often been cited as conclusive
proof that the quantity of rain was thereby diminished,
after examining the question with much care, remarks :

" In my judgment it is settled that very large clearings must diminish the annual fall of rain in a country."

Numerous other authorities might be cited in support
of the proposition that forests tend to produce rain ; but
though the arguments of the advocates of this doctrine
are very plausible, not to say convincing, their opinions
are rather *a priori* conclusions from general meteorological
laws, than deductions from facts of observation, and ↓

is remarkable that there is so little direct evidence on the subject.

The effect of the forest on precipitation then is not free from doubt, and we cannot positively affirm that the total annual quantity of rain is diminished or increased by the destruction of the woods, though both theoretical considerations and the balance of testimony strongly favor the opinion that more rain falls in wooded than in open countries. One important conclusion, at least, upon the meteorological influence of forests is certain and indisputed: the proposition, namely, that within their own limits and near their own borders, they maintain a more uniform degree of humidity in the atmosphere than is observable in cleared grounds. Scarcely less can it be questioned that they promote the frequency of showers, and if they do not augment the amount of precipitation, they equalize its distribution through the different seasons.

It is frequently asserted by dwellers upon the Plains that a perceptible change has taken place in the climate since the introduction of railroads and the settlement of the small portion of territory already occupied. Intelligent men express their full conviction that rainfalls are more frequent, and the climate generally is less liable to sudden changes and extreme variations than formerly. It is hardly within bounds of possibility, however, that any essential change can have been effected by the settlement of a portion so insignificant in comparison with the whole area. The following interesting extract from a letter I have recently received from Mr. Wm. N.

Byers, Editor of the Rocky Mountain News, in reply to an inquiry on this subject, probably furnishes the most rational explanation of the belief which is frequently expressed. Few men have had as good opportunities of observation as Mr. Byers, as he has lived for more than twenty years between the Missouri and the Pacific; for a very large portion of the time in the open air, and since 1856, with the exception of occasional interruptions, has been furnishing meteorological reports to the Smithsonian Institute. As the records have to be made daily, and at certain hours, the effect could hardly fail to systematize his observations and give much greater weight to his opinion than to that of a merely casual observer.

It will be seen that his idea of the effect of forest planting, in modifying the climate by checking the winds, whose "exhaustive power" is a chief cause of the aridity of the Plains, corresponds with that which I have elsewhere expressed. He admits that wherever trees are planted and nourished into mature growth, "they ameliorate the climatic condition immediately around them," and that the protection they afford arrests and preserves humidity by checking evaporation. This corresponds with the conclusions I have elsewhere quoted, viz: "that within their own limits and near their own borders they maintain a more uniform degree of humidity than is observed in cleared grounds." If this is true, it follows that a sufficient proportion of forest would secure the desired effect, even though no increase was wrought in the annual amount of rainfall."

"With twenty years observation on the Plains I unhesitatingly give it as my opinion that there is no change in their climatic laws. I think there is a perceptible but irregular cycle of years, progressing from extreme wet to extreme dry, and the reverse, but nothing else. I account for the "mere opinion of old settlers," to which you refer, as follows : These old settlers came from the East — from moist, and, more or less, humid climate ; ordinarily having frequent and often excessive rains ; a dense, sticky soil. The change to a country of exact opposites was very impressive. They noticed it most the first year because so different. Memories of the old were fresh ; inconveniences of the new exaggerated. As the former faded from year to year, the latter were surmounted one by one. Gradually he adapted himself to the new order of things. Ditches, water, irrigation, bring verdure. Trees spring up ; they ameliorate the climatic condition immediately around. With shade, and green grass and gurgling streams, the "old settler's" discomforts disappear as the memories of former years fade in oblivion. Hence his opinion, in which he is as honest as though it was a fact.

"I know how common it is. I meet the assertion or the inquiry almost every day. In vain do I cite the history of Eastern lands, where they irrigate to-day as they did three thousand years ago, else gather no harvest ; of Western South America ; of Mexico, old and new ; of California, peopled by our own citizens, where they have suffered for two years the worst droughts in twenty-four.

" Forest planting will modify and ameliorate our climate, *because*, to *start* the forest, water *must* be provided. The same supply that nourishes the tree, brings grass or other verdure. The former breaks the wind (one day's wind is more exhaustive of moisture than three day's sun), the latter carpets and protects the earth. The little rain that falls, instead of being immediately absorbed by and from the bare, sun-parched and wind-lashed earth, goes to the tree and grass roots, and for hours or days will cool the shaded air. The tree requires less water the second than it does the first year. Its demands diminish year by year, until finally its roots will have struck deep enough to supply all its wants. The water supply that will enable the planting of an acre of forest trees this year may safely be

extended to half an acre more next year; to an additional three-
quarters of an acre the next, and so on. Could forest planting be
made *general* it might in time affect the laws of climate over a wide
area — might *possibly* increase perceptibly the rain fall — but I have
no hope of that. The farmer, or the·neighborhood, may greatly
improve his or their surroundings, but the general laws of the universe
can hardly be changed by man's feeble hand.

" I have traveled nearly a thousand miles south of here among
fields and vineyards that have been cultivated for three hundred
years; have witnessed their wonderful productiveness and seen above
and beyond the irrigating ditches that watered them the most
parched and utter barrenness. Even the mountain sides produce no
trees. The valleys are densely populated, and if rain was to follow
man, certainly it would have come to bless them."

Without seeking further evidence, or discussing the
question, whether the effect of forests is to create a
change of climate by electrical or chemical action, or is
merely mechanical, it is obvious that they do render cultivation possible, and exert an influence in retaining
humidity in their immediate vicinity. It follows that the
extent of this influence will be proportionate to that of
the area on which forest growth is secured, and this is
the most encouraging fact connected with the subject,
since it relieves us of the appalling necessity of waiting
till a large portion of the whole area is covered with
forest before hoping for a perceptible change.

It is hardly possible for the mind to grasp the idea of
so vast an extent as is comprised in the area of the great
Plains; and it is idle to talk of attempting within any
appreciable time to plant trees enough on a tract which
in its transverse section is five hundred miles across, to
produce a climatic change. But it is certain that every

such improvement brings its own reward in its immediate vicinity, and the only successful solution of the problem of converting the plains into arable and habitable lands, is through the medium of forest planting. Settlement and civilization are absolutely impossible without providing timber for the wants of the settlers. Railroads may be built as the Pacific railroads have been, by the constant efforts of construction trains in bringing forward supplies from the rear. But it has already been shown that the natural supplies of the older regions are running short of the demands upon them, and it is idle to suppose that they can be relied upon for the wants of a new country nearly as large as the whole region between the Mississippi and the Atlantic coast, which is entirely bare of trees. But even if it could do so, the cost of transportation of all the timber required for the infinite variety of purposes of domestic use, to say nothing of fuel, would be such as to prevent the possibility of settlement except in the comparatively few localities where an investment of capital was warranted by special objects. The class of pioneers who are usually the first to develop the agricultural wealth of a new country, and whose labor and productions are the foundation of its prosperity, could gain no foothold in a region which, whatever might be the capacity of its soil, is destitute of the timber which is essential to its settlement and cultivation. Until this want is supplied, therefore, the region in question must form a natural barrier, or line of separation, instead of a connecting line between the eastern and the western portions of the country, contributing by its resources and its wants to the active commercial intercourse of each.

How much of the region is capable of growing timber at all; how much of it requires irrigation to insure successful culture, and how much consists of alkaline deposits on which no culture is possible, are questions to which only vague and indefinite replies can yet be made. But of this simple fact we may be assured, that very extensive tracts, which are capable of forest culture, and which at present may be said to possess no intrinsic value, are now accessible by the Pacific railroads.

We know that the belt of prairie has its greatest transverse expansion in the Missouri basin, and that east of the meridian of Fort Laramie, the prairies are covered with rich grasses adapted to pasturage, which for an unknown period have supported countless herds of bison.

Where such grasses will grow, trees will grow, and with the growth of trees in sufficient quantity will come the increase of humidity and the modification of the storms, floods and other excesses of natural phenomena, which are fatal to the success of extended agricultural operations. The first step toward the settlement of the country, therefore, should be the planting of tracts of forest wherever it is practicable along the line of railroad, or elsewhere; and the first thing to be ascertained is, what varieties of trees are best adapted to such culture. Probably it may be impossible at first to grow some of the varieties most desirable for timber; but if we cannot have what we would, let us have those we can. Plant those that *will* grow, and in time they will serve as screens for more valuable kinds, as is done on the sea shore, where the worthless silver poplar (abele) will grow luxuriantly and in a few years form a screen behind which more delicate deciduous and evergreen trees will grow as readily as if they were unaware of the vicinity of the ocean.

The labors of Mr. R. S. Elliott, Industrial Agent of the Kansas Pacific Railroad, have thrown much light upon the subject, and his own report of them contains so much interesting and valuable information which ought to be widely disseminated, that I insert the whole of it. I visited Mr. Elliott's nurseries in the summer of 1871, and made a careful examination of all the varieties of trees under culture, and my observations enable me fully to corroborate his interesting statements.

EXPERIMENTS IN CULTIVATION ON THE PLAINS ALONG THE LINE OF THE KANSAS PACIFIC RAILWAY.

BY R. S. ELLIOTT.

[Published in Prof. Hayden's Geological Report.]

The treeless plains between the Platte and Arkansas Rivers may be said to extend from the ninety-seventh meridian of longitude to the Rocky Mountains. North of the Platte and south of the Arkansas the general features of the country are similar, but for the purpose of this report we need only have in view the region between the rivers. Its drainage is mainly through the Kansas River, the numerous affluents of which afford, in pools or currents, the water-supplies which have enabled the buffalo to sustain himself in all its parts. Along some of the streams there are occasional groves and fringes of timber — ash, box-elder, cedar, cherry, cottonwood, elm, hackberry, oak, plum, walnut, and willow; some of the species persistent to the mountains, but not in numbers or distribution sufficient to change the character of the country from that of open, treeless plains, rising gradually from about 1,000 feet above the level of the sea at the ninety-seventh meridian to more than 5,000 feet at Denver.

There is great uniformity in the surface of this immense inclined plane. The face of the country presents a series of gentle undulations, but there are no points of much elevation above the general surface, nor any great depressions below it. The geology seems to be in harmony with the surface features, as the earths and rocks of this vast region, five hundred miles in width, range from Lower Cretaceous, (Mudge,) on its eastern border, to the later Tertiaries of the Lake period, (Hayden and Newberry,) near the base of the mountains.

Open on the north to the arctic circle, and on the south to the Rio Grande, with no mountain ranges or extensive forests to check atmospheric movements, the great plains must necessarily be swept by winds as freely as the ocean. In spring and summer the winds from the southward are most prevalent. In winter the winds are more frequent from the northward. In the autumn they are apt to be more variable, and at the same time of more gentle character. Wind from the west is seldom observed. The winds are often strong, but they cannot be classed with destructive gales. They come with a steady pressure, which may cause a frail building to tremble, but will not overturn it. Tornadoes and hurricanes seem to be unknown. There is no record or tradition of such manifestations. Local thunderstorms and heavy rains, over comparatively limited districts, are experienced as detached phenomena, but are apt to be incidents of a storm covering a large area, and moving eastward. Days of comparative calm and of gentle breezes often occur, when, perhaps, for a week the windmill is unable to work the pump at the water station, but total rest of the atmosphere, except for brief periods, is rare. The climate is propitious to health and to comfort ; for although changes of temperature are at times sudden and considerable, yet injurious results seldom follow them.

As we pass westward from the ninety-seventh meridian, the atmosphere is observed to be more arid. Within two hundred miles of the mountains, the deposition of dew is at times so light as to be of little or no service to the vegetation. The annual rainfall is also less as we go westward, decreasing nearly in the ratio of distance until the divide is reached at and southwest from Cedar Point, in which vicinity there is supposed to be more rain than eastward in the plains or westward nearer the foot-hills. The natural effect of decreasing precipitation and increasing aridity is in some degree shown in the vegetation. The grama and buffalo grasses continue, together with the sunflower, *solanum*, *euphorbia*, and other plants, which are vigorous, nearly if not quite as far east as the ninety-seventh meridian ; but we find that the blue-joint grass of Central and Eastern Kansas is less abundant, and that *cleome*, *ipomea*, cactus, *artemisia*, etc., enter

on the more arid scene as if in their chosen home. But no considerable part of the plains between the Platte and the Arkansas is so arid
as to be destitute of vegetation, although the change in the flora
is rather distinctly marked as we pass from the middle of Kansas
westward.

Like any other extensive area, the plains exhibit a variety of soils,
but the fertile greatly exceed in extent the unfertile districts. Loam,
with greater or less mixture of vegetable matter, is the prevailing soil,
the proportions of sands and clays differing greatly in different localities. The patches of sand or gravel of meager fertility, or of alkaline
clays, unsuited to general plant growth, are very small in proportion
to the whole area, and with irrigation in some parts, and without it in
others, the entire region would prove, on trial, to be productive, with
as small a share of waste land as some of the most favored States.
The value of the plains for production is more affected by peculiar-
ities of climate than by poverty of soil.

EXPERIMENTS IN CULTIVATION ORDERED.

Twenty years ago the lands available for general agriculture west
of the State of Missouri were supposed to lie in a belt of not more
than one hundred miles in width, extending north and south. Even
when the Territory of Kansas was organized, the whole area west of
Missouri and east of the mountains was of doubtful value in public
estimation ; and emigration was stimulated by political considerations
rather than by correct knowledge or appreciation of the country.
Beyond the narrow belt, and stretching away to the mountains, was
the unfruitful waste, as popularly estimated. Its possible future usefulness for pastoral purposes had been at times suggested, but the
day for its actual occupancy, if ever to arrive, was regarded as far
distant. The settlers, however, soon ventured beyond the supposed
boundary of productiveness ; and as they increased in numbers, the
area of available lands was found to extend itself westward, as if to
meet their necessities. The construction of the railway brought
increased emigration, more accurate knowledge of the resources of
the country, and a firmer confidence in its future. By 1870 settle-

ments had stretched along the railway to points more than two hundred miles west from the State of Missouri. The pioneer had passed the boundary of the traditional "desert" at the ninety-seventh meridian, and in his march westward had found that the desert, like its own mirage, receded before him. Was his march to continue ; and how much farther could soil, temperature, and rainfall be relied on to reward cultivation ? These questions, important to the interests of the general public, as well as of the railway, could best be answered by experiments, and the directors of the company ordered some such experiments to be made.

In the spring of 1870, gardens were made at some of the stations, at distances between two hundred and thirty-nine and three hundred and seventy-six miles west of Kansas City ; the farthest westward being at Carlyle Station, 2,948 feet above the level of the sea. Seeds tried in these gardens germinated well, and the plants, with rude and imperfect culture, grew encouragingly. The results were satisfactory, although the destruction by insects was greatly beyond anticipation. Irish potatoes, for example, made vigorous growth, yet about the time of blooming were destroyed by a species of blister-beetle, (*Epicauta corvina*, Riley,) which proved to be a more formidable enemy than even the Colorado potato-bug. Spring wheat matured merchantable grain at Carlyle.

In the summer and fall of 1870 a few acres were broken at each of the three following stations, on the Kansas Pacific Railway, distant from Kansas City and above the level of the sea as follows :

Stations.	West from Kansas City.	Above sea-level.
	Miles.	*Feet.*
Wilson, (now Bosland).............	239	1,586
Ellis	302	2,019
Pond Creek	422	3,175

These places are in the western half of the State of Kansas. All are in the present buffalo range ; all are in the region of short grasses ; all are in the open, treeless plains, beyond the limits heretofore assigned to settlements.

Wheat, rye and barley were sown at each of these stations in the fall of 1870 ; at Pond Creek, September 28 ; at Ellis, October 20 ; and at Wilson, November 11. At Pond Creek the rye grew finely and matured a fair crop ; the wheat and barley were partially winter-killed, but the surviving plants made heads of the usual length, well filled with grain of good size and quality. At Ellis the promise of all the grains was excellent until the 1st of June, when a hailstorm of unusual severity prostrated every stem. At Wilson the grains all did well. The President a d the Secretary of the Missouri State Board of Agriculture (who, in company with members of the board, visited the stations in June) say in their report : " We found wheat, rye, and barley sown November 11, 1870, (at Wilson,) equal to if not beyond the average crop of any part of the Union." And of Pond Creek they say : "The rye, sown 28th of September, on raw ground, would rate as a good crop in Missouri or Illinois ; and of the winter wheat and barley, the plants which had survived the winter were heading out finely. Rye may be regarded as a valuable crop to the west line of Kansas (without irrigation) ; and further trials of wheat and barley of the more hardy kinds will, in all probability, be successful."

Trials of grass seeds at the stations named have shown that sorghum, lucerne, timothy, clover and Hungarian grass may be regarded as future forage crops on the plains ; the first and last being the most promising. Maize can be grown for fodder at each of the stations, and for its grain at Wilson and Ellis. At Pond Creek, sorghum made a good length of stalk and matured fine panicles of seeds. At Ellis and Wilson the stalks reached a height of nine to ten feet, and abundance of seeds were matured. This plant will be found to be of great value in Western Kansas and Eastern Colorado, if its usefulness for fodder has not been greatly overrated. In the dry atmosphere of the plains, the stalks could probably be dried so as to avoid the souring of the juice, on which account, in Illinois, an objection has been raised to its use as a fodder-plant.

TREE-SEEDS.

There were planted at Wilson tree-seeds as follows :

FALL OF 1870.— Ailantus, chestnut, oak, peach, pecan, piñon.

SPRING OF 1871.— Ailantus, catalpa, elm, locust, honey-locust, silver-maple, osage-orange, walnut.

All these seeds, except the piñon, (nut-pine of New Mexico, *Pinus edulis*,) have done remarkably well.

Seeds of ailantus, catalpa, locust, honey-locust and osage-orange were tried at Ellis with encouraging prospects, when most of the seedling trees were destroyed by the hailstorm of the 1st of June. Seeds of ailantus, sown broadcast during the first week in June, came up well, and the little trees came safely through the summer.

Seeds of ailantus sown at Pond Creek resulted in a moderate growth of trees, of which a large proportion survived the summer.

The experiments with tree-seeds, though very limited, have sufficed to show that trees may be grown from seed without irrigation, to the west line of Kansas, and in all probability to the base of the mountains.

Cuttings of cotton-wood, Lombardy and white poplar, and white and golden willow, were tried at Wilson and did well in that locality. Cuttings of cotton-wood and the willows were also tried at Ellis with a measure of success.

TRANSPLANTED TREES.

Trials were made at Wilson of transplanted trees of the following kinds :

EVERGREENS.

White pine _____*Pinus strobus.*
Scotch pine_____*P. sylvestris.*
Austrian pine _____*P. Austriaca.*
Corsican pine_____*P. Laricio.*
Norway spruce _____*Abies excelsa.*
Red cedar _____*Juniperus Virginiana.*

DESIDUOUS.

Ailantus ------------------------------------*A. glandulosa.*
Ash--*Fraxinus Americana.*
Box-elder------------------------------------*Negundo aceroides.*
Catalpa ------------------------------------*C. bignonoides.*
Chestnut ------------------------------------*Castanea vesca.*
Cotton-wood ------------------------------*Populus monilifera.*
Elm--*Ulmus Americana.*
Honey-locust----------------------------------*Gleditschia triacanthus.*
European larch------------------------------*Larix Europea.*
Linden ------------------------------------*Tilia Americana*
Silver-maple ------------------------------*Acer dasycarpum.*
Sycamore-maple ----------------------------*A. pseudo-platanus.*
Osage-orange----------------------------------*Maclura aurantiaca.*
Lombardy poplar----------------------------*Populus dilatata.*
White poplar----------------------------------*P. alba.*
Tulip tree ------------------------------------*Liriodendron tulipifera.*
White willow ------------------------------*Salix alba.*
Golden willow--------------------------------*Salix alba* (var).
Walnut--*Juglans nigra.*

The foregoing trees, whether transplanted or from seeds or cuttings, have done well at Wilson, making growth equal to what is usual in Eastern Missouri or Illinois. Rev. E. Gale, one of the regents of Kansas State Agricultural College, examined the trees on the 18th of August, and reported measurements as follows :

FROM SEED.— Ailantus, 24 to 30 inches ; catalpa, 3 to 12 inches ; chestnut, 4 to 12 inches ; elm, 10 to 20 inches ; locust, 36 to 48 inches ; honey-locust, 16 to 24 inches ; silver-maple, 12 to 24 inches ; oak, 8 to 10 inches ; osage-orange, 12 to 30 inches ; peach, 24 to 30 inches ; pecan, 4 to 9 inches ; walnut, 10 to 12 inches.

FROM CUTTINGS.—- White poplar, 12 to 27 inches ; Lombardy poplar, 24 to 36 inches ; cotton-wood, 18 to 24 inches ; white willow, 24 to 36 inches.

TRANSPLANTED.— Ailantus, 48 to 60 inches ; ash, 10 to 16 inches ;

box-elder, 36 to 40 inches ; catalpa, 12 to 24 inches ; chestnut, 8 to 14 inches ; cotton-wood, 36 to 60 inches ; elm, 20 to 30 inches ; honey-locust, 36 to 42 inches ; larch, 6 to 12 inches ; linden, 9 to 18 inches ; silver-maple, 24 to 30 inches ; sycamore-maple, 12 to 24 inches ; osage-orange, 12 to 36 inches ; peach, 30 to 36 inches ; white poplar, 24 to 36 inches ; Lombardy poplar, 24 to 36 inches ; tulip-tree, 8 to 10 inches ; willows, 36 to 48 inches ; walnut, 6 to 8 inches.

Mr. Gale says : " The evergreens have nearly all lived, and have made a growth of from 4 to 8 inches. All have done well. There is certainly nothing in the appearance of these trees to discourage the planting of evergreens in Kansas." It is proper to state that the cat-alpa-seed was sown broadcast on ground which had been broken the November previous, and was not replowed. Seedling walnuts were grown by putting the seed under fresh turned sod. None of the trees had the care or cultivation usual in nurseries.

At Ellis the same transplanted trees were tried as at Wilson, except red cedar and cotton-wood. The result was encouraging, although the chestnut, larch and Norway spruce may be said to have failed on this first trial, and some others were less vigorous than at Wilson. The hailstorm of 1st June greatly damaged the trees, cutting off the leaves and shoots and splitting the bark ; yet a large portion of the deciduous class made a fair growth, and about 50 per cent. of the pines survived. Of ailantus, ash, catalpa, honey-locust and white poplar planted at Ellis, every tree survived, and nearly all of the box-elder, elm, silver-maple, osage-orange, Lombardy poplar and black walnut.

At Pond Creek the growth of some kinds of trees was highly encouraging. Ailantus, ash, box-elder, catalpa, honey-locust and osage-orange have done best, and promise well for the future. Elm and black walnut made moderate growth, and seem to have estab-lished themselves. The willows, the poplars, and the silver-maple did not come up to expectation. European larch and most of the evergreens failed ; but a few of the pines lived through the summer, and in another season will probably do well. The trees at Pond Creek are in one of the most forbidding spots of all the plains. At the new station, Wallace, about two miles eastward, and on higher ground but with different soil, silver-maple and Lombardy poplar seem to do much better than at Pond Creek.

NO IRRIGATION.

The experiments were all without irrigation. Except to soak some of the seeds, or to puddle the roots of the trees as they were set out, not one drop of water was applied by human agency. The trees had not the benefit of good care and cultivation ; they were not aided by mulching the ground ; nor had they any shade or shelter from the winds. All the conditions of the experiments were such as the ordinary farmer may easily imitate.

One object was to test the possibility of growing trees and other plants on the plains depending on the rainfall alone. It was deemed important to show that the settler in the open waste may adorn his home with trees ; may grow fruits and timber ; may raise grains and other vegetable food for his family and his live stock without resort to expensive processes of artificial watering. So far as we may judge from a single season, the object has been accomplished ; and it is not doubted that future years will sustain the promise of the past season.

SETTLEMENTS ON THE PLAINS.

Within the past two years settlers, in families and colonies, have spread westward, along the line of the Kansas Pacific Railway, and also on streams north and south of the road, nearly to the one hundredth meridian. The purpose is generally to grow and deal in cattle and other live stock, and this purpose will be greatly aided by the capability of the country to produce grains and other products of general agriculture. The first settlers keep near the streams, as a general rule, for the convenience of water ready at hand and the limited supply of timber. If we look backward twenty-five years and reflect on the westward extension of settlements during that time, we must see that the causes which have pushed the "frontier" nearly three hundred miles west from the mouth of the Kansas River, are yet in active operation, aided by potent agencies not then in existence. *Then* the locomotive was unknown west of the Mississippi ; *now* there are in Iowa, Missouri, Nebraska and Kansas thousands of miles of railroad. *Then* the entire population of the United States was only about twenty-one millions ; *now* it is over forty millions. It is safe to say that the forces operating to throw population westward, taking into consideration facilities of transportation, are three times as powerful as they were twenty-five years ago. The result will be a gradual spread of people over the great plains, arranging their pursuits and modifying their habits to suit the capabilities of the country and the necessities of their respective localities.

EFFECT ON CLIMATE.

It is a bold assumption to say that the spread of settlements over the plains is to materially affect the climate. Yet it is not unreasonable to expect a degree of amelioration. Every house, every fence, every tree which civilized communities may in the future establish in those vast, open areas, will aid, in some measure, to check the sweep of the winds. Every acre broken by the plow will retain a greater amount of moisture after rains, and for a longer time, than the unbroken prairie. The genial rains of spring and summer will evaporate with less rapidity, and there will be a greater degree of humidity in the atmosphere, heavier dews, and possibly more frequent showers. Even if the annual average of rainfall shall not be increased, the chances are that it will be more evenly distributed. If we may judge by the experience of other parts of the world, where the destruction of forests has operated to dry up fountains, we may reasonably expect that the breaking up of the surface by the plow, the covering of the earth with taller herbage, and the growth of trees, will all tend to the development of springs where now unknown, and to render streams perennial which are now intermittent. Thus the gradual spread of inhabitants over the plains will tend to enlarge their capabilities and to render them more habitable.

Under date of June 10th, 1872, Mr. Elliott writes me as follows :

" We have planted a variety of seeds and have up — at Wilson — butternuts, coffee bean, box elder, hickory, locust, honey-locust, osage-orange and black walnut.

" At Ellis — the same except coffee bean — also, white ash is up.

" At Pone Creek — Box elder, locust, honey-locust.

"Ailantus is up at Pond Creek and Ellis — at each place, larch planted this year looks well. Will succeed at Ellis. I have not been at Pond Creek for a month, and cannot report on it.

" Transplanted ash, catalpa, box elder, honey-locust, silver-maple, black walnut and osage-orange do well at Pond Creek and at Ellis. Pines are doing well at each place, but better at Ellis and Wilson than at Pond Creek. At Ellis, last year's pines (Austrian and Scotch), have made shoots eight or nine inches long.

" Corn, sorgum, millet, pumpkins, potatos, melons, pea-nuts, etc., etc., are all doing well at Wilson and Ellis ; rye at Pond Creek ; rye and wheat at Ellis ; corn was doing well at Pond Creek, my men say, but was all pulled up by gophers or prairie dogs.

" At Wilson, a variety of trees and shrubbery sent by Thos. Meehan, of Philadelphia, are doing well — spireas, altheas, forsythias, etc., also paulownia, mountain ash, hornbeam, judas tree, etc.

" The experiments will go on this year, not in a large way, but sufficient to prove a great deal. The Railroad Company is only *testing*, but it is something to have even a small test going on. All who examine the little fields are surprised. Other railroads are operating. The Atchison, Topeka & Sante Fè Railroad Company has made arrangements with S. T. Kelsey to plant part of a section every ten miles west of the 99th meridian.

"You may safely say that tree culture on the plains is possible, without irrigation."

It will be seen that Mr. Elliott's efforts have been directed to prove that the growing of trees is possible, even with the slight care they are likely to receive at the hands of the average pioneer settler. No irrigation was made use of, and no cultivation was applied after the trees were planted. The experiments were the more valuable on this account, as proving that it involved no extraordinary outlay of capital or labor. And it is the more encouraging from the evidence it affords that the careful culture which should be bestowed wherever the work of forest planting was systematically undertaken would be amply rewarded.

The question naturally arises, by whom are these plantations to be made? The United States Government is obviously the party most largely interested, being the largest proprietor, and the lands being at present almost valueless for want of timber, yet susceptible of attaining an enormous value within twenty or thirty years, by a judicious system of forest planting. A company has recently been organized in Kansas, which comprises the names of several very able and reliable men, who propose to commence and carry out an extended system of forest planting if they can get from Congress a grant of land sufficient to warrant the undertaking. They ask a grant of one section of land for every mile, from Fort Dodge, Kansas, to Pueblo, Colorado, — 270 miles — and propose to plant eighty acres of forest on every section, and to make an experimental station every few miles, for the purpose of testing every variety of tree that could be of any practical value to the country for fruit, ornament, fuel, timber or shelter. The wisdom of giving liberal encouragement to such enterprises is manifest, and at the outset it is essential that government aid should be extended. After the system is once fairly inaugurated it will prove self-supporting and work its own extension.

The following circular has been issued by the association, and comprises an interesting statement of the necessity of the work and the means by which they propose to begin it :

"The design of the association is to settle the great question so often asked, " *What are these barren plains good for?*" by investing capital, skill and labor, in the experiment on such a scale as will, if successful, increase the value of *three hundred thousand square miles* of territory, vastly more than the small franchise asked from the Government is worth ; for in its present condition it is an unprofitable and unproductive *area.* Our association is duly incorporated under the laws of Kansas, and our board of directors are all men who have been closely identified with the subject of tree growing for years. Three of our directors, Dr. Warden, of Ohio, Robert Douglass, of Waukegan, Illinois, and Prof. S. T. Kelsey, of Pomona, Kansas, are men of *eminent ability* and *experience* in tree growing, and have a national reputation as scientific horticulturists, having made this business a life study.

"Prof. Kelsey has the immediate supervision of all the forest tree growing of the association, assisted by the experience and advice of Dr. Warden, of Ohio, and Mr. Douglass, of Illinois. Hon. Alfred Gray and J. K. Hudson, of Wyandotte county, Kansas, both of them members of the State Board of Agriculture, with Hon. W. H. Smallwood, Secretary of State, are directors in the association, and are all experienced horticulturists. The President of our association is Col. T. J. Peter, General Manager, of the A. T. & S. F. Railroad. Every member of this association is heartily in sympathy with the proposed enterprise, and if Congress will give us the encouragement asked for, we expect to make the solution of this question a leading one for the next five years.

"We are now engaged in a series of experiments between Topeka and Fort Dodge, on the lands of the Atchison, Topeka & Santa Fè Railroad, and if Congress will grant us the aid asked for, we propose to continue our work across the plains, by investing capital, skill and

energy in this enterprise, which will add directly and indirectly millions of dollars to the value of our Government possessions in the
West. THESE LANDS ARE AT PRESENT WORTHLESS, and unless the
requisite assistance is rendered to prove their capacity for agricultural developments, millions of acres of them MUST REMAIN OF NO
VALUE WHATEVER.

" Our association is composed of men who have faith in believing
that *their* practical experience, coupled with *their* great interest and
sympathy with this subject in all its bearings, can and will, (if encouragement is given us,) give to these lands a value a thousand times
more than the franchise asked for are worth to the General Government.

" West of the Mississippi there is not a State that has a stick of
timber more than is needed for its own consumption in our own
generation. The Sierra gorges, and a large surface of Oregon have
good supplies of timber, and some of the mountain ranges are well
covered with trees, but no streams *are there*, large enough to convey
the logs or lumber to where it is needed, or can be made available.
FIVE ACRES OF GOOD TIMBER, selected and cultivated where it is needed, is of more value than five hundred acres away where it cannot be
made available for our purpose.

" The American forests, once the richest inheritance that Divine
providence ever bestowed upon a people, have been swept away before the onward march of civilization, to such an extent, that it has
already become a question of serious import, ' WHERE SHALL THE
SUPPLY FOR FUTURE GENERATIONS COME FROM ?' No rational answer
can be given to this, other than to enter immediately upon the work
of Forest Tree growing. This is imperatively necessary, both for
protection in exposed situations, and for building and mechanical
purposes.

" With the present and prospective increase in the consumption of
pine, all the accessible pine timber east of the Rocky Mountains will
soon be exhausted. The Chicago market alone receives over one
thousand millions of feet of lumber per annum, and say that this
represents *one-fourth of all* the lumber that is taken from our forests

in one year, and you can plainly see that the aggregate will very soon cause the last "Requiem of the Pine Forest" to be sung, for in twenty years they will all have melted away. INDIVIDUALS, STATES and NATION should awake to the fact that soon our whole forest supplies will have passed away. The only remedy is in a system of forest growing, aided and encouraged by Government, and unless this *is* done, *we will soon be compelled to resort to importation.* There is no place on the continent where the encouragement of a completely organized system of tree planting, by men who thoroughly understand the business, and appreciate the great and growing necessity for the inauguration of these and kindred enterprises, will be of SO GREAT A NATIONAL BENEFIT as on the barren plains of the West. It would convert *this vast desert* into a well developed agricultural country more rapidly than anything the Government could do, and we believe the subject is one well worthy of the care and attention of Congress.

"The Hon. J. M. Edmonds, the commissioner of the public lands, in his report to the House in answer to the enquiries of Hon. J. M. Donnelly, in regard to this question of forest tree growing, says under date of May 29, 1866:

* * * * * * * * * * *

"'The subject of inquiry is one of vast importance to the future of this country, a proper answer to which can only be made after exact knowledge shall be gained as to the best and surest means of promoting the purpose in view.

"'A large portion of the vast region between the Mississippi and Pacific is wholly destitute of timber, and this destitution is the great and principal hindrance to the RAPID ADVANCE OF SETTLEMENTS.

"'These vast treeless plains and plateaus WILL BE RENDERED HABITABLE ONLY BY THE PRESENCE OF TREES AND GROVES, which will fertalize and moisten the soil, soften and modify the climate, and protect men and animals from the blighting effects of dry and searching winds which now almost desolate that region.

"'It is a demonstrated fact that POPULATION WILL NOT AND CANNOT ADVANCE FAR BEYOND THE PROTECTION AND ADVANTAGES OF GROVES AND FORESTS. In densely timbered sections, trees in the opening of the country are the great obstacles to improvement and cultivation, and are therefore destroyed, not only without mercy, but with zest and with utter disregard of the future.

*　*　*　*　*　*　*　*　*　*

" ' Already the great forests of New York, Pennsylvania, Indiana and Ohio have been so far depleted that those States resort to Michigan and Wisconsin for lumber and timbers for domestic use. True, those States have yet much timber, but they have little or none of the most valuable kinds for export, and they have so well learned its value that they will purchase rather than use their own, preferring to hold it as an investment.

" ' But how long will the forests of Michigan, Northern Wisconsin and Minnesota stand before the treble drain of the older Eastern States, the great prairies and the valley of the Mississippi? Long before Michigan, Northern Wisconsin or Minnesota, (the only States which can now export timber in large quantities,) shall contain a population one-half as dense as Massachusetts, they will not only cease to export, but will find a scarcity for their own local purposes.

*　*　*　*　*　*　*　*　*　*

" ' It should be borne in mind that to this time our great forests have met the demands and destruction of a gradually rising population from three to thirty-three millions of people, whilst they were for nearly the whole time diving deeper into the recesses of the unbroken primeval supply. We have now gone through and surrounded this great timber reserve, and we enter upon the margin of the great treeless waste with our original store three-quarters consumed, the demand accelerated, and the consumers to rise rapidly from thirty-three to fifty millions within the last third of this century. A little common arithmetic will satisfy any thinking man of the consequences, and of the proportion which the demand and supply will bear to each other at the close of as compared with the commencement of this century. Extend the time for another five years, with the added population, and it will be fortunate if our people get boards three inches wide, as in China at the present time. Is it not apparent that we should at once cease to destroy and commence to produce?'

9

"Here we have the views of a gentleman who has given the subject much thought and attention, and his views should be received as coming from a source entitled to credit.

"We ask the aid of the Government, because we look upon this work as being of NATIONAL IMPORTANCE and this experiment on such a scale as to be of permanent value, requires the outlay of a large amount of capital, from which no return can be expected for years, and without the aid and encouragement of Congress, the amount of capital necessary to carry it forward cannot be enlisted.

"We do not expect to raise forests to supply the necessities of the country, or to meet the demands of the future, but we propose to make such experiments, and on such a scale, as to show how it can be done, and publish the results of our successes and our failures to the whole country, so that all may be benefited by them.

"NO ONE INDIVIDUAL CAN AFFORD EITHER THE LAND, THE LABOR OR THE NECESEARY EXPENDITURES OF MONEY TO MAKE THESE EXPERIMENTS, and hundreds of men who are willing to plant forest trees on the plains, are waiting to profit by the experience and expenditures of others who must first point out the proper way and kinds to plant. When the experiments are properly made and the necessary information given, *there will be plenty to imitate.* Every tree grown by our association, or that by our example and influence may be grown, will be just where it is wanted, and where it will do the most good. Our association will not only be obliged to expend vastly more than what these lands are worth to carry on this enterprise successfully, but will in addition have to expend a large portion of the lands also in order to get the necessary labor located where it will be available for our use, and what land we can save, and the growth of our trees, will be our reward for capital and labor expended. If we are not successful in growing these trees, the Government loses nothing by the work we do. Almost any other expenditure, in any legitimate enterprise, will yield a speedy return — commerce, manufactures, crops or herbs — *but in the planting of trees it will be years before* the profits for skilled labor and capital expended will show any return. *No great and complete efforts have ever yet been made with a view to ascertain definitely what use can be made of this vast area of treeless lands.* Some persons, it is true, have planted a few trees on the plains, but nothing scientific or systematic, designed to establish facts and principles in this direction, has ever yet been undertaken.

"It is a well known fact that *forest trees exercise a grand influence* (when they are present) over the climatology of the country, and control to a great extent climatic extremes. They are beneficial to the agricultural interests around them. Rains are induced by them, springs are created in the thirsty land by their planting, and the cold blasts of winter are moderated by them.

"'*Is there an interest so great that is so much neglected* — one so much needing attention as this?' Government is liberal in its donations in the interest of commerce, and as the full development of the agricultural interests of the land is the true basis of National wealth, our law makers should be equally liberal in fostering and protecting so vast an interest. 'Is there any better way to encourage *a measure of National importance* than by aiding an enterprise that will develop so great an interest, as the one proposed in this bill?'

Yours most respectfully,

E. S. NICCOLLS,

Secretary Western Forest Tree and Hedge Growing As., of Kansas."

Next to the National Government, the parties most interested in the work are the various railroad companies whose lines intersect the region, and whose extended territorial possessions would be vastly increased in value by the establishment of an extended and wisely managed system of forest planting. The advantages they would thus secure, have already suggested themselves to the directors, and the subject has been more or less agitated for two or three years past, but I have not yet heard of any decisive action on the part of either of the great companies. The Kansas Pacific led off by the appointment of Mr. Elliot as Industrial Agent, and the establishment of experimental nurseries; but after proving the possibility of growing trees as far west as Pond Creek, 400 miles west of Kansas City, they have left it to others to profit, if they will, by their labors, but have failed to turn the knowledge thus acquired to their own benefit. The Atchison, Topeka & Santa Fè Railroad has made an important move in the right direction by a liberal arrangement with Mr. S. T. Kelsey, one of the most experienced and reliable tree planters of the West, who is to plant a certain portion of each of twenty-eight sections of land, situated ten miles apart on the line of the road. The trees are to receive what attention they require till they attain such age and size as to need no further care — the object being to demonstrate the possibility and the profits of forest culture, as an encouragement to settlers. The Burlington & Missouri River Railroad has had a good deal of discussion of the subject of forest planting on the line of the extension of the road from Plattsmouth to Fort Kearney, along the whole of which route, tree culture, I am confident, would be perfectly easy; but no definite results have followed. If the Union Pacific has taken any steps in the matter I have heard nothing of it, and the Northern Pacific, I am informed, " has not done much in the way of planting trees, except commencing the work along the line for wind-screens and snow-breaks."

The work is of a novel character, involving very considerable outlay, and promising no immediate return. It is also extraneous to the usual customary works incident to railroad direction, and has therefore an apparently speculative character which directors are unwilling to assume.

The Leavenworth, Lawrence & Galveston Railroad Company, under the direction of its wise Superintendent, O. Chanute, Esq., has instituted a system for the purpose of encouraging settlers along its line, in planting hedges, which is well worthy the consideration of many other roads.

The nature of this system may be best explained by the following circular, which is sent to every land proprietor along the line of the road :

SUPERINTENDENT'S OFFICE L., L. & G. R. R., }
LAWRENCE, KANSAS, November 8, 1871. }

The killing and injuring of stock by trains, proving not only a great loss and annoyance to farmers along the line, but a source of considerable danger to the trains and the traveling public, the Leavenworth, Lawrence and Galveston Railroad Company is desirous of beginning the fencing of its line in advance of any legal requirement to do so, and for this purpose makes the following proposal to the proprietors of the land adjoining its right of way :

1. The railroad company will, upon application, furnish at the nearest station, during the proper season for planting, osage orange plants in sufficient quantities to set out a hedge on the right of way lines through each cultivated farm, and will, when the hedge is grown and in condition to turn stock, as ascertained by actual examination of a skilled inspector, pay the proprietor, or his assigns, the sum of thirty-five cents a rod.

2. The railroad company will, about the time the hedge is ready to turn out to stock, fence up at its own expense such short gaps as must be necessarily left where there is no soil to grow a hedge, and will

connect the same with the bridges, cattle passes and cattle guards.

3. The company will, upon application, put in such new cattle guards as may be required to enable the farmers to protect the growing hedges by cross fences or other field enclosures ; the necessity to be determined by the company.

4. The proprietor or tenant of the land shall prepare the same for setting out the hedge, and the plants will not be furnished until the inspector has examined it and reported it to be in good condition.

5. All setting out, protecting, cultivation and care of the hedge shall be performed by the proprietor or tenant, and the above mentioned payment of thirty-five cents per rod, shall only be made when it is a continuous efficient hedge, capable of turning stock of all kinds, save at those points where there is no soil, as above provided. The intent of this proposition being to throw the whole care of the growing hedge upon the farmer, and to make it to his interest to do the work well.

6. In order to prevent the entire failure of any piece of hedge once started, the company reserves the right of taking charge of any portion of the same which may be abandoned or improperly taken care of by the farmer. In which case he shall be entitled to no compensation for setting out or cultivating the same ; but the company shall only be entitled to take possession of the same after three disinterested fence viewers, selected from among neighboring farmers. shall have decided that the hedge is not receiving proper attention.

7. As experienced hedge growers in this State estimate the whole cost of preparing the ground, setting out and raising a hedge, the plants being furnished, at from twenty to twenty-five cents per rod, it is hoped that the higher price here offered will induce proprietors to enclose and cultivate the land near the railroad, so as to avail themselves of this proposal.

8. Any benefits or bounties provided by the laws of the State for growing hedges will be relinquished by the company to the farmers.

9. Forms of contracts, made assignable upon the sale or transfer of the land, have been prepared, embodying the above conditions, and will be filled out upon application being made in writing upon the

form herewith. Blanks may be obtained from the section foreman, or from the station agents.

10. As it is very desirable that the company should know at an early day how many plants to provide for next spring, the farmers who may wish to avail themselves of this offer are earnestly desired to fill out and forward their applications without delay. Make out a separate application for each piece of land, even if owned by the same party, so as to avoid the making out of new contracts, should you hereafter sell a portion of your land.

The company will not be bound to recognize any application made subsequently to the first day of March, 1872.

O. CHANUTE, *Superintendent.*

With the circular the farmer is also provided with a printed blank for him to fill, stating the location of his land, how many rods of hedge will be required on each side of the railroad, and how much of it he will have in readiness for planting the ensuing season. This is accompanied by a printed envelope, directed to the superintendent, labelled "Application for Hedging," in which the blank form, after being filled, may be enclosed and left at the nearest railroad station, to be forwarded to the superintendent's office. A form of contract is then sent to him to be signed, binding him and the company to the mutual performance of the duties set forth in the circular, and at the proper season the requisite number of hedge plants are forwarded. This method of relieving the farmers so far as possible of labor and inconvenience in making the application, has no doubt tended greatly to promote the success of the work; and I am informed by Mr. Chanute that the farmers respond to the call with hearty interest, and applications were received during the winter, and have been since filled, for more than sixty miles of hedging.

Without going deeply into estimates, whose results would be dependant upon many contingencies, it is not difficult to prove by very simple calculations that the future interests of every road which crosses the plains are so intimately connected with the work of tree planting that it cannot afford to forego the advantages it offers. As I selected the item of ties as the simplest article with which to illustrate the amount of timber consumed, let us again make use of it as a basis of calculation of possible results.

Seedling larch trees of two years growth can be had at the nurseries for $5 per 1,000. If set in nursery rows, the plants being a foot apart, and three feet between the rows to allow room for culture with a horse-hoe, an acre would contain about 14,500 plants. From year to year the alternate plants, and after a time the alternate rows, should be transplanted, till an average of 400 trees to an acre was attained, when the original occupants of the single acre would cover about forty-three acres. In fifteen years from the time of first planting every tree would furnish, at least, one tie. Supposing every alternate tree to be then cut we should have 7,250 ties. Five years later every remaining tree would furnish two ties (14,500), making in all 21,750 ties in twenty years from time of planting.

The following is an estimate of the cost:

Original cost of 14,500 plants at $5 per 1,000.............$ 72 00

Culture for six years (after which they may be left to themselves), say $100 per annum_____   600 00
                                                   _____
                                                     672 50
Interest on the above for twenty years at 10 per cent._____ 1,345 00
                                                   _____
         Total cost of 21,750 ties_____$2,017 50

This makes the cost of the ties less than ten cents each,
but it will be observed that I have not included the cost
of cutting and hewing, or sawing them out.   I believe that
if the work were undertaken in the comprehensive and
liberal manner which the truest economy would dictate,
the proportionate cost of all the items of culture would
be reduced to such a degree, and might be so relieved by
sales of crops grown in the intermediate spaces that the
cost of the ties need not be more than the sum I have
stated.   Hickory and oak saplings are fit for hoop poles
at six or eight years, and cedar, larch, spruce and fir are
valuable for fencing stuff at eight or ten years.   These
should be planted liberally with those which are to remain
longer, and their sale would materially diminish the costs.
But suppose that no such aid were received, and we allow
the cost of cutting and hewing to be twenty cents for each
tie, the sum would then be thirty cents each, which is less
than half their present price, which certainly cannot
diminish unless some new invention supersedes them.

I am very confident that by judicious management their
final cost might be reduced to a less sum than my estimate, if not entirely cancelled.   An expenditure of thousands *now* may save a future imperative necessity for the

outlay of millions. But of course such a work requires the exercise of thoughtful care and judicious management.

A general superintendent should be appointed who should unite the characteristics of a thorough man of business and a competent nurserymen. His first work should be the selection of a position for the primary nursery, which should be fully appointed with all necessary buildings, teams, wagons, tools and implements for thorough and extensive nursery culture. The whole work of propagation from seed or cuttings should be performed here, and from this point the secondary nurseries, which should be established at every station along the line of the road, should receive their supplies of young trees. These secondary nurseries could be managed by intelligent laborers accustomed to such work, and would, of course, be under the supervision of the superintendent, who should visit them as often as necessary and direct their general management. It should be a special object, at the earliest possible moment, to render the stations attractive by tasteful plantation of trees and shrubbery in their vicinity, by which I mean not merely planting a few trees and shrubs in a yard adjoining the station, but a tasteful disposition of groves and groups on conspicuous surrounding points and hillsides. The effect upon the mind of travellers, of such an oasis in the desert, is cheering and refreshing beyond conception, and in no way could the capacity of the country for tree culture be so successfully demonstrated. Every station thus adorned, with its nursery adjacent, would become the nucleus of a settlement ; the opportunity of providing themselves on

the spot with trees, being in itself a strong attraction to
settlers. If the mode of supplying them, and the conditions which should be insisted upon to insure proper
planting and culture I shall speak hereafter, but before
approaching that subject I wish to say a few words on the
mode of planting which should be adopted.

Mr. Elliott's experiments afford valuable suggestions
as to the kinds of trees which are likely to prove most
hardy, and which should therefore be most liberally used
as screens on the sides which most need shelter. Some
of these varieties would not be available so far north as
the line of the Northern Pacific, but I think the ailantus,
cottonwood, box elder, (negundo,) and white ash would
prove as reliable as in Kansas, and should therefore be
liberally used at the outset for screens. They should occupy the summits of ridges and prairie swells, and the
more tender varieties should be planted on the northern
and eastern slopes. This arrangement may surprise
those who are not familiar with the subject, whose first
impression would be that a warm southern slope should
be selected for such purpose, but I feel warranted in the
assertion by long experience and observation of facts.
The prevailing wind all over the country, which blows
with the greatest violence and with the longest duration
is from the S. W. — and it is the wind whose parching influence is most detrimental to vegetation. I have been
surprised to find what a comparatively small number of
persons have observed, (till their attention has been
called to it), the striking evidence of this truth, which is
afforded by the attitudes of trees in exposed situations —

leaning, or with a decided tend of the branches and spray toward the northwest. From Maine to Colorado, and from Minnesota to Texas, one need never be long at a loss for the points of the compass, who has learned to observe this effect, which after a little experience becomes so familiar that he detects it intuitively.

Sometimes every tree, for a large space, will have a decided lean — sometimes individual trees only exhibit the effect — and sometimes the branches are compressed toward the trunk, on the windward side, and spread away from it on the other, while the trunk itself is not affected. The explanation is simply that the season at which the S. W. winds prevail with greatest frequency and violence, is during the spring and early summer, when the tree is full of sap, and the young shoots are easily bent, and have not yet attained sufficient elasticity to recover their natural position. During many years that I was largely engaged in fruit growing in New Jersey, I learned to dread this wind as the worst enemy of my crops, and the one whose attacks were especially to be guarded against. Further observation since has served to prove that the influence of these winds is much more widely extended than I at that time imagined, and a very important fact in regard to the modification of their effects, by passing over large bodies of wood or water does not seem to me to have received the attention it merits. Wherever the S. W. wind strikes upon the land after passing over a large body of water it tends to ameliorate the climate as compared with that of places in the same parallel of latitude with a different aspect towards the water. On a large scale this may be seen by comparison of the East and West coasts of Continents. Europe receives the S. W. winds from the Altantic, and we find the vine and olive growing in the latitude of Boston, which is that of central Spain and Italy. Follow the same parallel to our Western coast and we find in California growing luxuriantly the fruits which in Boston can only be raised under glass, and with artificial heat.

The same effect, in a less degree, may be observed when the expanse of water is very much less. At Newport, R. I., as is well known, many plants are found to flourish, which in the interior cannot be grown north of Philadelphia. In Nova Scotia (which, like Rhode Island, receives the S. W. wind directly from the ocean), the English ivy thrives without protection, which in Boston — two degrees farther south — is annually killed to the ground. It is common to attribute this to the influence of the gulf stream, but the same result is found on the shores of the great lakes. The whole eastern shore of Lake Michigan, from St. Joseph to the Grand Traverse region, is the land of the peach and the grape, and of a luxuriant forest vegetation. The S. W. wind has a sweep of sixty miles across the laĸe before striking the shore, and the result is that for all purposes of cultivation the country is the same as the region about Philadelphia, while the whole western shore from Chicago northward, is utterly incapable of producing the more delicate fruits, and the native forests are comparatively confined to a limited number of varieties, and those of stunted growth. The influence of wood land upon temperature is of the same character as that of a

body of water, and so far as opportunity has favored observation, its benefits are conferred under similar relative
conditions.   The parching effect of these winds sweeping
unobstructed over the vast extent of the plains, after being robbed of what moisture they might previously have
contained, in their passage across the mountains, is sufficient to account for the lack of vegetation, and wherever
the attempt is made to restore the soil to a cultivable
condition, the first step should be to counteract their
blighting influence.   The ridges and uplands should
therefore be planted with such varieties of trees as are
found most hardy and least affected, and the Northern
and Eastern slopes thus protected, might then be planted
with those requiring shelter, with great certainty of successful results.   If the slopes were roughly terraced, as
they might be, with a plow, at no great cost, the object
would be greatly promoted, by the more permanent re-
tention of the moisture from rainfalls.   As an additional
aid to this end, wherever possible a thorough system of
mulching should be adopted.   Few persons, even among
the practical horticulturists, are aware of the value of
this process, when properly performed.   I have seen
it practised extensively on coffee plantations in Cuba, and
have myself applied it to vineyards and pear orchards in
New Jersey, with surprising results.   But what I mean is
a very different process from simply mulching around each
tree in a circle equal to the extent of the branches.   The
whole ground must be covered, to a depth sufficient to
prevent the growth of weeds and grass, to supersede the
necessity of cultivation between the rows, and to retain

the moisture of the rainfalls for a great length of time, preventing the heating and baking of the earth, and effecting the same object which in the natural forest is secured by the annual fall of the leaves. No one who has not witnessed the effect can realise the amazing difference in the health and vigorous growth of trees thus treated, in comparison with those where the ground is left bare. Wherever it is possible to procure material for the purpose, it should be applied. Doubtless a great deal might be procured in the sloughs and swales of the prairies by mowing the rank grass and rushes which grow in such places, and with railroad transportation at command, it would not be difficult to procure very large annual supplies from swampy tracts wherever they occurred along the line, and deliver them at the stations where they were wanted. An experienced Cincinnati grape grower told me some twenty years since, on seeing the effect of such an application to my vineyards, in New Jersey, that he was richly paid for his journey by what he had learned of the value of the operation.

The primary nursery should be devoted exclusively to propagation and experimental cultivation. The secondary nurseries should receive annually from the primary a stock of young trees, not over three years old from the seed, sufficient to keep up their supply to a fixed standard to be determined by the demands upon them, which would be constantly increasing. These trees should remain at least one year in the secondary nursery before being sold to settlers or removed to the point where they were permanently to remain. I shall speak presently of the supplies for settlers, which will require a very large quantity. But beside those, there should be annually planted a certain proportion of the land owned by the railroad company, on each side of the line. Of course it is desirable that this should be as large as possible, provided the planting and culture is properly attended to. The work should be extended from year to year and from section to section of the lands belonging to the company. The planting should be systematically done. A portion of every section should be reserved for the express purpose of growing timber for future use by the railroad itself. This would naturally be on the side nearest to the railroad. On the rest of the tract the plantations should not be continuous, but in groves, selecting as far as possible the northern slopes and summits of ridges, and leaving the southern slopes for cultivation.

The effect of scattered groves as shelters and windscreens would be much greater than that of continuous wood, while it would be much more attractive to purchasers, since it would make a more convenient arrangement of tillage and wood land, reserving the most desirable portions for the former purpose. The details of arrangement of the plantations would of course be directed by the superintendent, who it is to be presumed would be thoroughly acquainted with the work. A moment's reflection will show that there is great room for the exercise of judgment in adapting varieties to conditions of soil, and in making such disposition of them as to secure returns at the earliest possible moment.

For instance, it would be very desirable to make large plantations of white pine, for future supplies of timber. But the white pine is of no value in its youth, in fact is hardly worth cutting till it is forty or fifty years old, and does not come to maturity till seventy-five, and in order to get the best timber the trees should be ten or fifteen feet apart. But this of course is unnecessary during their early years, and the intermediate space may be filled with hickory, oak, ash, cedar, spruce and larch, which may be removed and sold for hoop-poles, fencing, posts and railroad ties, at different periods from six to twenty years of age, by which time the pines would have attained a size sufficient to require all the ground, while the previous thinnings would have yielded an income sufficient to pay a handsome interest on the value of the land for the time when it otherwise would have yielded no return.

The above general process of extending the forest plantations should be going on from year to year in the vicinity of every station, and for lands thus planted a proportionately higher price should be demanded.

In addition to these plantations made by the railroad itself on its own lands before offering them for sale, a system should be adopted for furnishing every settler with a certain number of trees, proportionate to the amount of land purchased by him of the company. These should comprise an assortment of fruit and forest trees and shrubs, and should be put at the lowest price at which they could be afforded. They would add but slightly to the price per acre in the purchase of a quarter section, and it would doubtless prove an attractive feature in the advertisements of the company's lands if emigrants were informed that fruit and ornamental trees enough to stock the farm would be included in the purchase at so much an acre.

Of course the nursery would be open to all customers, but no one could complain at the preference shown to purchasers of railroad lands.

It is not improbable that professional nurserymen might be found who would be glad to contract with the company to take charge of the whole work, the railroad furnishing land for the primary nursery, and facilities of transportation; and the nurseryman furnishing stock and agreeing to plant a certain amount of forest annually and attend to its culture, and also to supply to every settler a certain amount of fruit and forest trees, proportionate to the amount of his land, to be paid for by the company. This method might on some account be deemed preferable, but I do not think the results would be likely to be as satisfactory as the other, though the point of vital importance is the personal character and capacity of the one in charge. If he is an honest man of efficient executive ability, and familiar with the practical requirements of the work, it will be likely to be well done, whether he takes it on contract or as an employed superintendent. The work is so vast and involves so much which must be learned by experiment, that it is hardly possible that any one can escape errors, and it is all important that the unavoidable difficulties should not be complicated by inefficient management and false economy. If the work

is undertaken carelessly, without the preparation of a
general system and organization, it may accomplish
nothing beyond the expenditure of a large amount of
money with no satisfactory results. If, on the contrary,
it is begun and prosecuted in a wise and liberal spirit —
proceeding cautiously in cases of doubt, and with all the
energy of abundant force when doubt is removed — there
need be no apprehension that the result will not be commensurate with the magnitude and grandeur of the work,
whether considered merely as a pecuniary investment for
the benefit of the stockholders, or as a national benefit
by the conversion of an uninhabitable desert into a
region of agricultural wealth capable of supporting a
dense population. Whether as a means of attracting
settlers and adding to the value of their lands, or of
providing timber for their own future wants, and the
demands of roads which in time will certainly intersect
the country in every direction, it is obvious that to forego
the advantages which may thus be secured, is indicative
of a "penny wise and pound foolish" policy which is
inconsistent with the energy and enterprise which resulted
in the construction of the trans-continental railroads.